ZEPPELIN L15
&
THE WAKEFIELD GOLD MEDAL

ZEPPELIN L15 & THE WAKEFIELD GOLD MEDAL

PUBLISHED by Bernard A. N. Green

ISBN 978-0-9576042-2-3

Printed by Biddles Books, King's Lynn, Norfolk, PE32 1SF

Acknowledgements

This book would not have made it to the printers if it was not for my wife Peggy who put up with me ignoring her wishes while I sat at the computer for many hours.

I should also like to acknowledge the invaluable information compiled by RJ Sirley for his article published in *Medal News* in 1982.

Finally, I should like to thank my friend Graham Spicer for his advice and help with formatting the manuscript and for undertaking additional research.

Author's Note

This is a privately published, low volume, not-for-profit book intended solely for educational purposes. Although it is believed that the images used are copyright free or do not infringe copyright for the purpose stated above, the author should be notified of any exceptions and shall be pleased to remove these, or provide acknowledgement of source, in any updated edition of this work.

This volume is a compendium of three booklets I have written on World War One Zeppelins:

Part 1

ZEPPELINS THAT BOMBED LONDON
An easy to read guide to the Zeppelin raids on Great Britain, and particularly London, during the Great War.

Part 2

ZEPPELIN L15 & THE WAKEFIELD GOLD MEDAL
The story of how Sir Charles Wakefield, the Lord Mayor of London, discharged a personal debt of honour when London was under attack from Zeppelins.

Part 3

THE STORY OF THE LZ85 COMPASS
How a chance find in an antique shop uncovered a little known piece of World War One history.

"These are true stories about the airships that were built to wage war, the men who flew them and those who shot them down."

CONTENTS

LIST OF ILLUSTRATIONS

PART 1 - ZEPPELINS THAT BOMBED LONDON

THE ZEPPELINS

Since warfare began the only effective way to defeat an enemy nation had been to invade their homeland or lay siege to it and starve them into submission. All this was about to change, however, with the advent of the Great War in 1914. This would be the first human conflict in which a strategic bombing campaign would be used to attempt to defeat another country.

This new type of warfare would subsequently be refined to unleash mass destruction, resulting in many civilian deaths, during World War Two and most conflicts thereafter. During the Great War air raids were still in their infancy but the concept was terrifying to most people at the time who were shocked that an enemy could strike from afar in the dead of night and kill them in their beds.

It was Germany that took the lead in this new type of warfare with its advanced airship technology. Great Britain trailed second placed France in this respect. Inauspiciously, the first British airship, built by aeronaut Stanley Spencer, was flown 30 miles (48 km) from Crystal Palace in South London to Ruislip, on 22nd September 1902, carrying an advertisement for baby food. Arguably, the greatest contribution made to the Great War, by British dirigibles, was their use as U-Boat spotters for the Royal Navy.

Fig 1. ***Submarine Scout Zero (SSZ) Type Airship number 37 flying above a Royal Navy minelaying vessel***

Germany, in the meantime, had been developing the rigid airship design of Count Ferdinand von Zeppelin, first flown in 1908, with some success. Although most people identify Great War airships with the name Zeppelin, successful rigid airships were also developed by another German manufacturer from 1909, the Luftschiffbau Schütte-Lanz Company, formed from a partnership between Professor Johann Schütte and Dr Karl Lanz.

The principal difference between the two types of airship was that the Zeppelin used a high strength aluminium alloy duralumin frame, invented in 1909 by Alfred Wilm, while the Schütte-Lanz was constructed from wood. Unfortunately the latter, whilst offering potentially superior performance to the Zeppelin, was susceptible to wet weather which caused distortion and weakening of the structure.

The German Army favoured the Schütte-Lanz while the Navy preferred the Zeppelin.

Germany's exploitation of airships in the Great War was driven by an alliance of just three men; Count Ferdinand von Zeppelin, creator of the Zeppelin, Korvettenkapitän Peter Strasser, Commander of the German Naval Airship Department, and Airship pioneer Dr Hugo Eckener, civilian director of airship training for the German Navy. Eckener, an early associate of von Zeppelin and senior advisor to Peter Strasser, trained more than 50 flight crews over 1,000 men in total. After the Great War, he remained a lifelong advocate of the benefits of airships for passenger travel.

Fig 2. ***Dr Hugo Eckener with Count von Zeppelin and Korvettenkapitän Peter Strasser***

Zeppelin numbers may sometimes appear confusing as each had two numbers; a military number and a maker's construction number. If one takes the **L15/LZ48**, as an example, L15 is the German Naval number and LZ48 is the maker's construction number.

A number of different Zeppelins were built and used during the Great War. These comprised the M,N,O,P,Q,R,S,T,U,V,W and X Classes. Three M Class Zeppelins were used in the first raid on England in January 1915. These had open gondolas, which resulted in great hardship for the crew. This was rectified with the P Class which had enclosed gondolas, to protect the crew, but it was still extremely cold at altitude. The P, Q and R Class Zeppelins were potentially the most used, during the period 1915-1916, when the German bombing campaign against England was at its peak.

The P Class Zeppelins were first used in April 1915. They were 536.2ft (163.4m) in length and 61.3ft (18.69m) in diameter with a volume of 1,126,389 cu ft (31,895.8m^3) and 16 gas bags. They were powered by four Maybach 210hp (160kW) engines with a maximum speed of 60.1mph (96.7km/h), a cruising speed of 39mph (63km/h), a range of 1,336 miles (2,150km) and an operational ceiling of up to 12,000ft (3,658m) depending on weight and outside air temperature. The P Class had a crew of 19 and was armed with 7 or 8 machine guns. Two guns were mounted, one each side, on the forward control gondola. Two further guns were mounted, one each side, on the rear engine gondola with a further gun mounted in a small cockpit in the stern behind the rudders. Finally, two, or sometimes three, machine guns were mounted on top of the hull, which was reached by a ladder from the forward control gondola. The nominal bomb load was 4,400lbs (2,000kg). The P Class was the first Zeppelin used to attack London.

The Q Class was a lengthened version of the P Class at 585ft (178.3m) with a larger gas volume of 1,359,435cu ft (38,494.9m^3) and four Maybach 6-cylinder 240hp (179kW) engines. This specification, although it had a slightly reduced top speed of 58.9mph (94.8 km/h), provided a greater operational ceiling and bomb load.

The R Class, or so called 'Super Zeppelins', appeared for the first time over England in July 1916. They were 649.4ft (198m) in length and 78.4ft (23.9m) in diameter with a volume of 1,950,112cu ft (55,221m^3). They were powered by six Maybach 240hp (180kW) 6-cylinder engines which could generate a maximum speed of 63.8mph (102.7km/h), with a range of 4,600 miles (7400km) and an operational ceiling of 13,000ft (4,000m). The R Class had a crew of 21 and was armed with 10 machine guns. The nominal bomb load was 61,600 lbs (27,721kg). Four R Class Zeppelins, **L31/LZ72**, **L32/LZ74**, **L33/LZ76** and **L34/LZ78** were launched in 1916, but all were destroyed by the end of that year.

The S Class Zeppelins, first used to raid the British mainland in March 1917, were known as the 'Height Climbers'. As British air defences improved, throughout 1915 and 1916, the German Navy decided that an increased operational ceiling, allowing airships to operate at altitudes well above British fighters and Ack-Ack fire, would allow them to take back the initiative. This increased ceiling was achieved by reducing the weight of the S Class Zeppelin allowing altitudes of over 20,000ft (6,100m) to be attained. Unfortunately, the benefits of flying above the British air defences were offset by the freezing temperatures and lack of oxygen. Crews wore special cold weather clothing but this was barely sufficient to stop them freezing. Of greater concern was hypoxia caused by lack of oxygen. The crew could become dizzy and disorientated or even pass out. These challenges, both capable of mitigation by relatively simple technical solutions, were not clearly understood at the time meaning that the Height Climbers were not as successful as they might have been.

T, U, V and W Class Zeppelins followed with each type yielding a slight increase in specification and performance.

The last Zeppelins produced were the X Class in July 1918. The last raid on the British mainland in

August 1918, in which Korvettenkapitän Peter Strasser Commander of the German Naval Airship Department lost his life, was carried out by the X Class **L70/LZ112**.

The Schütte-Lanz airships, although not used extensively for raids on Great Britain, did play a part in the bombing campaign. A total of 21 airships, of Type 'b', 'c', 'd', 'e' and 'f' were constructed between 1914 and 1918 but not all were commissioned or saw active service. They were also powered by Maybach engines and had a similar performance to their Zeppelin counterparts. The most famous raid, by a Schütte-Lanz airship, was carried out by the **SL11** on London in September 1916. This was shot down by Lieutenant William Leefe Robinson, in a B.E.2c fighter, for which he was awarded the Victoria Cross.

Although airship development continued after the end of the Great War, the Hindenburg disaster in May 1937, in which 26 people lost their lives, marked the end of the airship era and a colourful chapter of aviation history.

THE RAIDS

The following is a summary of the historically significant Zeppelin and Schütte-Lanz airship raids on Great Britain, including London, between 1915 and 1918. The first Zeppelin raids were approved on the 7th January 1915 by the German Kaiser but raids on London did not commence until May 1915.

The First Zeppelin Raid on Great Britain

19/20th January 1915. The first Zeppelin raid on Great Britain was carried out by Naval M Class Zeppelins **L3/LZ24** commanded by Kapitänleutnant Johann Fritz and **L4/LZ27** commanded by Kapitänleutnant Count Magnus von Platen-Hallermund. The **L3/LZ24** dropped its bombs on Great Yarmouth while the **L4/LZ27** bombed Kings Lynn. M Class **L6/LZ31** had also taken off, to participate in the raid, but was forced to turn back due to technical problems at an early stage. The intended target had been Humberside which housed key industrial and military infrastructure but the resulting navigational errors resulted in a number of civilian deaths and injuries in East Anglia instead.

A total of four civilians were killed during the raids; Martha Taylor and Samuel Smith in Great Yarmouth and Percy Goat and Maud Gazeley in Kings Lynn. Their death certificates recorded cause of death as 'from the effects of the acts of the King's enemies', the first time this form of words had been used on the British mainland. A number of civilians were also injured, some seriously. The cost of the damage to Kings Lynn was estimated at £7,000.

The First Zeppelin Raid on London

31st May 1915. One of the P class Zeppelins, the **LZ38**, commanded by Hauptmann Erich Linnarz, who had undertaken a number of successful attacks on Britain in the preceding weeks, carried out the first bombing raid on London, killing 7 people and injuring 35, with property damage estimated at £18,596.

The first bomb dropped by the **LZ38** was an incendiary, which landed on 16 Alkham Road, Stoke Newington. This was the home of Albert Lovell, a 39-year-old clerk, and his family. The house was set alight but the blaze was extinguished by the Fire Brigade before it could cause serious damage.

Bombs were subsequently dropped on Dalston, Hoxton, Shoreditch, Spitalfields, Whitechapel, Stepney, Stratford and Leytonstone, during the raid, resulting in the deaths and injuries.

The civilians who lost their lives in the raid were:

Henry Good
Caroline Good
Elizabeth May Leggatt
Elsie Leggatt
Samuel Reuben
Lily Leahman
Eleanor Willis

The British B.E.2c fighter aircraft in use at the time were unable to reach the altitude that this type of Zeppelin could achieve. They were still vulnerable at lower altitudes however and Sub-Lt. R. A. J. Warneford was awarded the VC. for destroying the **LZ38** by dropping six 20 pound bombs, onto the top of the Zeppelin, when it descended to 7,000ft, over

Sint-Amandsberg in Belgium, on the 7th June 1915. He had followed it as it returned to its base.

The Most Destructive Zeppelin Raid on London

8th September 1915. The most destructive raid was carried out by P Class **L13/LZ45**, one of four Zeppelins that were deployed in the raid, commanded by Kapitänleutnant Heinrich Mathy a former destroyer captain. The **L13/LZ45** reached the British coast in East Anglia and turned south towards London.

When it reached London, the **L13/LZ45** dropped a total of 15 high-explosive and 55 incendiary bombs resulting in a fire that required 22 fire engines to control. A total of twenty-two civilians were killed and another eighty-seven injured. The resulting financial cost of the damage amounted to £534,287, which would be equivalent to more than £23,000,000 today.

Kapitänleutnant Heinrich Mathy flew several more raids on Britain but was killed on 2nd October 1916, when his new airship, the **L31/LZ72**, was shot down by Second Lieutenant Wulstan Tempest of 39 Squadron, Royal Flying Corps, in his B.E.2c biplane at Potters Bar in Hertfordshire. Mathy jumped to his death from the burning Zeppelin before it crashed into a field killing his entire crew.

Zeppelins Shot Down Over London

1st April 1916. The P Class Zeppelin **L15/LZ48**, commanded by Kapitänleutnant Joachim

Breithaupt, was hit by TRGA anti-aircraft guns at Purfleet near Thurrock to the east of London. It was then attacked by 2nd Lt. Alfred de Bathe Brandon RFC as it tried to escape over the North Sea, It was this action that resulted in the award of the Wakefield Gold Medal, sponsored by Sir Charles Wakefield the Lord Mayor of London, to all military personnel involved in the destruction of the Zeppelin.

2nd September 1916 The wooden framed Schütte-Lanz airship, **SL11**, commanded by Hauptmann Wilhelm Schramm was shot down by Lieutenant William Leefe Robinson. The Airship crashed in a field behind the Plough Inn at Cuffley in Hertfordshire killing Schramm and his fifteen man crew. Robinson, flying a converted B.E.2c night fighter no. 2693, used the newly developed Pomeroy incendiary ammunition.

Hailed as a hero he was awarded the Victoria Cross two days later. Not only was this believed to be the fastest award of a VC on record, Robinson was the first recipient for an action that occurred in Great Britain.

He was never comfortable with celebrity and returned to front line flying. Shot down, and captured in France, he spent the remainder of the war as a prisoner in increasingly poor health. He died on 31st December 1918 after returning to England.

23rd September 1916. The R Class Zeppelin **L33/LZ76**, commanded by Kapitänleutnant Alois Böcker, was damaged by anti-aircraft fire and then attacked and hit hit several times by night fighters from Hainault Farm. Credit for disabling the **L33/LZ76** was given to B.E.2c no. 4544 piloted by Lieutenant Alfred de Bathe Brandon who had been involved in downing the **L15/LZ48**. The **L33/LZ76** was forced to land at New Hall Farm, Little Wigborough, only twenty yards from a nearby house. The occupants of the house, the Lewis family, ran for their lives as the airship hit the ground.

Fig 3. ***The wreckage of the L33/LZ76 showing the close proximity to the Lewis family's home***

24th September 1916. R Class Zeppelin **L32/LZ74**, commanded by Oberleutnant-zur-see Werner Petersen, was shot down by 2nd Lieutenant Frederick Sowrey RFC, aged 23, from 39 Squadron at Sutton's Farm and crashed near Snails Farm, South Green, Great Burstead, Essex. Sowrey received the DSO for his actions.

2nd October 1916. R Class Zeppelin **L31/LZ72**, commanded by Kapitänleutnant Heinrich Mathy, one of the most feared Zeppelin commanders, was intercepted and destroyed by 2nd Lieutenant Wulstan Tempest near Potters Bar, just north of London.

Kapitänleutnant Mathy died after jumping from the flaming Zeppelin before his entire crew perished in the impact. The crew were originally buried at Potters Bar but were later exhumed and reburied at Cannock Chase. Tempest also received the DSO for his actions. The crash site is commemorated by a road named after him.

Fig 4. ***Three RFC Airmen who shot down Zeppelins***

The above photograph shows Lt. (later Capt.) William Leefe Robinson VC, 2nd Lt (later Maj.) Wulstan J Tempest DSO and Lt. (later Group Captain, RAF) Frederick Sowrey DSO posing together for publicity shot. The fact that RFC airmen were regarded as celebrities, while the Infantry were fighting a hard war in the mud, resulted in some resentment between the Infantry and RFC at the time.

The Last Zeppelin Raid on London

The final raid on London occurred on 19th October 1917. Flying higher than normal, at up to 20,000ft, the R Class **L45/LZ85**, commanded by Kapitänleutnant Waldemar Kölle, took the Capital by surprise, killing 33 people.

Seven were killed in Piccadilly, eleven in Camberwell and fifteen in Hither Green. The final bomb in Hither Green was the last one dropped on London by a Zeppelin. It almost wiped out the entire Kingston family.

The fifteen victims were buried in separate graves for the Catholics and Protestants. A memorial paid for by public subscription was erected, but, over time, it weathered and the names became increasingly illegible. A replacement was unveiled on 21st October 2017 at Brockley & Ladywell Cemetery.

The **L45/LZ85** escaped, but, with technical problems, was forced to crash land in south-eastern France where it was burnt by the crew before they were captured by the French authorities.

The Last Zeppelin Raid on Great Britain

The last Zeppelin raid on Britain took place on 5th August 1918 when four Zeppelins attempted to bomb targets in the Midlands and the North of England.

The Zeppelins were spotted by the Leman Tail lightship. Despite thick cloud hampering the defenders two aircraft intercepted the recently commissioned X Class **L70/LZ112** and it was shot down in flames, near Wells-next-the-Sea in Norfolk by Major Egbert Cadbury and his gunner Captain Robert Leckie flying a de Havilland DH-4.

Both men had shot down a Zeppelin previously; Cadbury had been credited with downing **L21/LZ61** on 28th November 1916 and Leckie **L22/LZ64** on 14th May 1917.

The remaining three airships dropped their bombs blind and these all landed in the sea. Most of the wreckage of the **L70/LZ112** was salvaged and provided a great deal of technical information. The bodies of the crew members were buried at sea.

Korvettenkapitän Peter Strasser, Commander of the German Naval Airship Department, who was on board the **L70/LZ112**, directing the raid, was also killed. His legacy would be long range air raids and inclusion of the civilian population as legitimate targets, both used to great effect by the German Luftwaffe in WWII. It was Strasser who famously said, *"We who strike the enemy where his heart beats have been slandered as 'baby killers'. Nowadays, there is no such animal as a non-combatant. Modern warfare is total warfare."*

Fig 5. ***Korvettenkapitän Peter Strasser, Commander of the German Naval Airship Department***

By 1917 Zeppelins had been mostly replaced by aircraft flying daylight raids, until losses became heavier, then night raids. The last Zeppelin raid on Great Britain took place in August 1918. The German Army had decided, as early as 1916 when the British developed incendiary ammunition, the use of airships was unsustainable but the German Navy remained enthusiastic to the last. There were 72 air raids on Great Britain, with over 50 of these on London, during the Great War, with 77 German Zeppelins out of their fleet of 115 craft destroyed or seriously damaged.

Between 1915 and 1918, according to official government figures, the German Zeppelin raids on London resulted in 557 fatalities and 1,358 injuries. The totals for the British mainland were 833 persons killed, and 2,002 injured. More than 5,000 bombs were dropped by Zeppelins across Britain resulting in damage estimated at well over a million pounds. Total air raid damage in the Great War, including by aircraft, was estimated at £2,900,000 with damage in London estimated at £2,200,000.

THE BOMBS

A mixture of incendiary and high explosive bombs were used. Many of the bombs were dropped by hand. They had handles at the top and the incendiaries, which weighed 25lb (11kg), were a mixture of Thermite and Benzole with tarred rope wound around the outside. This flammable material was used to create fires. High explosive bombs were also used. These varied in size but on 8th September 1915 the **L13/LZ45** dropped a bomb of 660lb (300kg) on London in what was the most destructive airship raid of the war.

THE GUNS

There were six hundred and twenty two searchlights and two hundred and seventy one anti-aircraft guns in Britain by the middle of 1916 including the twelve searchlights and thirty anti-aircraft guns in London.

In 1914 Britain had no anti-aircraft guns and initially London was defended against the Zeppelin threat by only four Pom-Pom guns on the roofs of the Crown Agents, The Foreign Office, The Admiralty and Woolwich Arsenal. These were mostly ineffective but served the purpose of boosting civilian morale. The Royal Arsenal in Woolwich was an armaments factory which was a high value target for attack by the Zeppelins. It was situated on the South Bank of the Thames and, at that time, covered a massive 1,285 Acres (520 Hectares). This was the reason that the Woolwich Battery was created to defend it. The factory finally closed in 1967.

The Pom-Pom gun had a calibre of 37mm (1.457 in). It was developed in 1897 by Hiram Maxim as a derivative of his rifle calibre machine gun. It was so named because of the sound it made on firing. A British version was developed by Vickers and Sons. The Germans also had their own version made by Mauser. The one pound weight of the projectile came about as a result of the Hague Convention of 1899 that stipulated explosive projectiles of less than 440g (15.5oz) could not be used against personnel. Although originally rejected by the British on the grounds of cost (six shilling per round) and calibre (too large for anti-personnel and too small for artillery) Vickers delivered 50 units and the weapon was adopted for anti-aircraft defence by the Admiralty in 1914. The generic term for these weapons was 'Ack-Ack' which was popularly believed to be as a result of the sound they made when firing. The real explanation was more mundane; 'Ack' was the phonetic alphabet word for 'A' at the time. 'Ack-Ack' was therefore the phonetic representation of 'A-A' which was itself a contraction of 'Anti-Aircraft'.

Fig 6. ***The Vickers Pom-Pom 37mm QF One Pounder on anti-aircraft mount***

The 'QF' designation stood for 'Quick Fire' and was of naval origin. For a gun to be classified as 'QF' it had to be capable of a sustained rate of fire of twelve rounds per minute, equivalent to one shot every five seconds. The gun could be manually operated, as long as it met this criterion, and didn't have to utilise an automatic or semi-automatic mechanism. The Pom-Pom 1 Pounder had a maximum range of 9,000ft (2,743m) so it could not reach the Zeppelins that flew at over 10,000ft (3,048m).

They were placed in London as a deterrent and to calm the fears of the residents of London. But the shells had a percussion fuze which meant they exploded on contact. If they hit the airship it was quite likely that they passed through without exploding and would fall back down onto London. They were fired in belts of twelve at a rate of sixty rounds per minute. The shell weighed one pound and one can imagine the effect of groups of twelve high explosive shells falling back down to earth in central London and exploding on impact.

Fig 7. ***The 37mm Pom-Pom shell MkII***

The above illustration is of a 37 mm Common fused Pom-Pom shell Mark 2 which has been cut away to show the interior. The top shows a screw which has a sharp point underneath which fires the detonator pellet on impact. The centre would contain 270 grains of F.G. explosive. The total length of the projectile and brass case was 6.6in (168mm). The propellant was cordite.

By July 1915 there were a total of eight of these guns in London. After September 1915 the pom-poms were removed, as the falling shells caused a lot of damage, at the same time the French 75mm (3in) anti-aircraft gun was being fitted to the mobile units.

Fig 8. ***French soldiers firing the 75mm anti-aircraft gun in Salonika, Greece during WW1***

Other anti-aircraft guns, used for the defence of London include the QF 9 cwt 13 pounder, based on a naval QF 3 inch design and the QF 18 pounder models. The 13 pdr was 3 inch calibre and the 18 pdr 3.3 inches. Both weapons were less than optimal for air defence, however, due to their low muzzle velocity.

Fig 9. ***QF 13 pdr 3 inch 9 cwt anti-aircraft gun***

This problem was solved by 1916 with the introduction of a 3 inch calibre gun, based on the 18 pdr, using a necked case from the 18 pdr fired through a 3 inch calibre sleeved barrel. The more powerful ammunition increased muzzle velocity dramatically and resulted in the creation of the QF 3 inch 20 cwt gun. This became the standard anti-aircraft gun for the defence of Britain with 202 out of 371 being of this type by the middle of 1916. The 9 cwt 13 Pounder and 18 Pounder were retained in use with 35 of the latter in use in 1916 and 56 at the end of the war.

Fig 10. ***QF 3 inch 20 cwt anti-aircraft gun***

Both fixed and mobile guns were used to defend Britain from the Zeppelins. Mobile Ack-Ack guns, mounted on lorry chassis, had been developed by the Royal Engineers at Fort Brockhurst, Gosport Hants. These mobile guns were driven by members of the Army Service Corps attached to the gun teams.

Fig 11. ***A British mobile QF 13 Pounder mounted on a 3 ton Daimler lorry***

Fig 12. ***A British QF 3 inch 20 cwt anti-aircraft gun mounted on a 4 ton Peerless lorry***

The Purfleet Ack-Ack gun, which claimed the Wakefield Prize, was positioned in August 1914 to protect the Royal Gunpowder Magazines which had stored and supplied gunpowder to the Navy and Army since the year 1760. The No. 5 magazine is now the Purfleet Heritage and Military Centre.

The Purfleet gun was situated adjacent to the site now occupied by Woodlands Pre-school and Nursery in Tank Lane, Purfleet Essex. This is commemorated by a blue and white sign on the wall of the building:

THURROCK'S HERITAGE

This high brick wall is part of the outer security defence of the Royal Gunpowder Magazines built in 1760. Close by was the large garrison water tank which gave its name to Tank Hill Road.

During the First World War anti-aircraft guns were mounted here to protect the Magazines. On the 31st of March 1916 shells from the guns crippled the Zeppelin LZ15 [sic] and the aircraft, which was 165m long, crashed into the Thames Estuary. This Zeppelin was the first to be brought down in Great Britain and the Lord Mayor of London gave the Royal Artillery gunners a gold medallion inscribed 'Well Hit'.

Anti-aircraft shells required a built in delay or fuze to ensure they exploded at the correct height. It could take up to 15 seconds for a projectile to reach the target. The Germans, who used clockwork fuzes, were more advanced than the British who still used ignitable fuze of the required length. This was facilitated by a Wilson-Dalby 'predictor', a device mounted on the gun, with the correct fuze length read off of a scale for the required target height.

Fig 13. ***Cutaway view of the British No. 80 time fuze used in Ack-Ack guns***

Interestingly the fuzes used by the British in their efforts to bring down the Zeppelins were invented by the German Krupp Company to whom Vickers paid royalties. These were suspended under the Trading with the Enemy Act. As a result of legal action, after the cessation of hostilities, the British eventually paid the Krupp company royalties for the use of its fuze technology during the war.

THE SEARCHLIGHTS

On 4th August 1914 Royal Engineers volunteers in the North East of England mobilised as the Tyne Electrical Engineers (TEE). No. 1 Company was stationed at Clifford's Fort on the Tyne, with responsibility of maintaining searchlights for coastal defence, while Nos. 2 and 4 Companies were based in Portsmouth, Hants at Haslar Barracks on the Gosport side of the harbour. The TEE took over the RE School of Electric Lighting at Stokes Bay near Gosport before the school's name was changed to the AA Searchlight and Sound Locator School and relocated to Ryde on the Isle of Wight. The TEE's base at Clifford's Fort on the Tyne remained their depot, however, until they eventually moved out in 1928.

By 1914 the London Electrical Engineers (LEE) had established six companies in their headquarters at 46 Regency Street, Westminster and searchlight units were deployed to the South Coast and Thames Estuary. The LEE, which had the nickname 'The Londoners', trained at the RE School of Electric Lighting in Gosport. They subsequently established a base at Streatham in the Borough of Lambeth. In 1915 the LEE created the Searchlight Experimental Establishment at Regency Street with a drawing office and workshops to facilitate searchlight development. This included new 90cm and 120cm electric searchlights and sound locators linked directly to the guns.

During September 1914, the War Office had handed the defence of London and anti-aircraft defence to the Admiralty. The guns were manned by the Royal Naval Volunteer Reserve and the searchlights by local special constables. In May 1915 there were 12 searchlights in London which were operated by 120 special constables. This equates to ten men per searchlight.

From December 1915 all the anti-aircraft (Ack-Ack) searchlight teams were provided by the RE London Electrical Engineers or Tyne Electrical Engineers. During the winter of 1915, Nos. 4, 6, 7, and 8 Ack-Ack Companies were mobilised by the London Electrical Engineers. The Royal Engineers controlled all anti-aircraft searchlights until 1938 when it was decided that they would become the responsibility of the Royal Artillery.

On the 16th February 1916 the War Office took control of the defence of London again. It appears that the first mobile anti-aircraft searchlight unit was created in London on the 11th March 1916, under the command of Major N. H. Firmin, was named No. 9 (Tyne) Mobile Searchlight Company TF RE. Each Mobile Brigade had six Ack-Ack guns. A Searchlight Company was divided into three sections, each having four searchlights. It was staffed by 7 officers and 138 other ranks which included 32 drivers of the A.S.C. Their equipment was 12 x 60cm searchlights transported on 3-ton Daimler Lorries. There were 6 motorcycles available for the use of officers. There were also 6 Fiat 30cwt Lorries used for stores and these were driven by 32 drivers from the ASC. There were 13pdr x 18pdr Ack-Ack guns. There were 7 officers in charge of 138 Other Ranks which included the 32 ASC drivers listed above.

The officers in this company were Maj. N. H. Firmin, Lt. T. Tucker, Lt. J.R. Abbott, 2nd Lt. J. A. Power, 2nd Lt. Lawther, 2nd Lt. J.Robinson and 2nd Lt. C. G. Huntley. From this Company detachments were sent out to defend what were considered vulnerable locations. One of these mobile detachments was based at Darenth, in Dartford, Kent. On the night of 31st March 1916 Kapitänleutnant Joachim Breithaupt had the misfortune to fly over them in the **L15/LZ48** as he was trying to escape towards the sea. They caught him in their lights, gunfire was then aimed at the **L15/LZ48** and they subsequently also put in a claim to the reward offered by the Lord Mayor of London Sir Charles Wakefield.

In 1915 night bombing by aeroplanes was almost unknown. Bombing by airships had been expected and it was felt that the 60cm searchlights would be effective enough to locate them, but they were not. So in 1916 the 90cm lights were introduced and at the same time the long arm method of controlling the direction of the light was developed.

In the autumn of 1917 mobile generating sets using the 120cm lights came into use. These mobile sets were much more complicated and required mechanics to have technical skills with motor vehicles and electrical systems.

By the middle of 1917 there were forty-two RE Ack-Ack searchlight companies in Britain. The following Army searchlight units were located in the London area by 1917:

- Nos1-6 Companies London Electrical Engineers (LEE)
- 11 AA Brigade Searchlight Company London Electrical Engineers (LEE)
- No. 12 AA Brigade Searchlight Company London Electrical Engineers (LEE)
- Nos 20 & 21 Aeroplane Squadron Searchlight Companies London Electrical Engineers (LEE)
- Nos 24-26 Aeroplane Searchlight Companies London Electrical Engineers (LEE)
- No. 1 Mobile Brigade, Tyne Electrical Engineers (LEE), HQ at Epping, with Nos 8, 9 & 10 Batteries
- No. 2 Mobile Brigade, Tyne Electrical Engineers (TEE), HQ at Sevenoaks, with Nos 7, 11 & 12 Batteries

At the end of WW1 there were approximately 3,000 all ranks in the service. Most of these were from the London Electrical Engineers and The Tyne Electrical Engineers. There were also a small number of men from The Royal Engineers. Of the 3,000 there were approximately 600 men, transferred from the infantry, who were medical category 'B'.

Fig 14. *A searchlight being assembled by a team of Royal Engineers territorials*

The searchlight units in the First World War were part of the Royal Engineers TF (Territorial Force) the equivalent of the modern Volunteer Reserve.

The long arm on the side of the light was introduced in 1917 to enable the man at the end to rotate the searchlight quickly and also change the angle of the beam with something like a steering wheel. Sound locators were introduced in 1918. Wills, the tobacco company, produced a series of cigarette cards featuring contemporary searchlights.

Fig 15. ***Wills cigarette card illustrating a mobile Searchlight in 1916 mounted on an Austin Lorry***

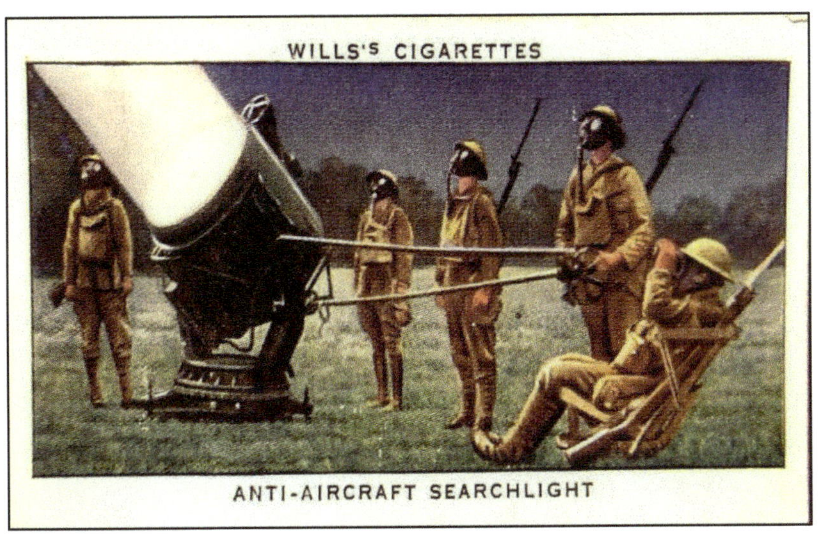

Fig 16. ***Wills cigarette card illustrating the arm used to control the direction of the light***

The crew are wearing their gasmasks.

Fig 17. ***Sound locators were used to listen for Zeppelins and enemy aircraft***

When the Admiralty originally took over the air defences for London in 1914, reporting was carried out in a rather random fashion by a number of different posts including police stations, railway stations, military establishments and lighthouses.

These were manned by members of the Special Constabulary, railway staff, the military and even boy scouts. Unfortunately, many of these posts were not connected by telephone or wireless and reporting could be erratic.

In 1916 the Army regained control of London's Air Defences from the Admiralty, against the latter's wishes, and one of the first changes was improvement of the aircraft reporting system. This was formalised by the creation of approximately 200 regular Observation Posts, connected by better communications, manned by the Special Constabulary.

This marked the establishment of the 'Metropolitan Observation Service' or 'MOS' which would evolve into the Observer Corps in 1925 before gaining the prefix 'Royal' in 1941 as a result of its outstanding service. The Royal Observer Corps was finally stood down in 1991 although elements lingered on until March 1996.

By the end of the war there were twenty-six RE Searchlight Companies, equipped with 622 searchlights, a mixture of 90cm and 120cm types.

Fig 18. ***RE and RGA personnel with a searchlight***

Fig 19. ***The famous poster showing a Zeppelin caught in a searchlight over London***

THE AIRCRAFT & ARMAMENTS

The mainstay of the British aerial response to the airships was the B.E.2c fighter flown by the RFC.

Fig 20. ***The British B.E.2c fighter***

The B.E.2 (Blériot Experimental 2) was originally designed by Captain Geoffrey de Havilland, who was also Chief Test Pilot, at the Royal Aircraft Factory in 1912. Later development, resulting in the B.E.2c, was undertaken by Lieutenant Edward Teshmaker Busk. The aircraft was a two-seater bi-plane which could be used in the capacity of interceptor, light bomber, flying trainer and reconnaissance aircraft. It's most famous role however was that of a single seater night fighter used to engage Zeppelins.

The B.E.2c wasn't ideal for this role as it was underpowered and its operating ceiling meant that most airships could increase their altitude to escape counter attacks. Despite this, airships were vulnerable when bombing as they needed to descend for accuracy. They were also susceptible to attack when taking off or landing and when in their hangars.

One of the most influential RFC squadrons, in the defence of London, was 39 (Home Defence) Squadron formed at Hounslow Heath Aerodrome (later London Heathrow Airport) in April 1916. The squadron's role was to counter the threat of Zeppelin raids on London. It had several outstations including Sutton's Farm near Hornchurch in Essex, (later to become RAF Hornchurch), and Hainault Farm near Romford in Essex. 39 Squadron was relocated to North Weald in August 1916. Its pilots were responsible for the destruction of three airships; the **SL11**, by Lt. William Leefe Robinson

(Sutton's Farm) on 2nd September 1916, the **L32/LZ74** by Lt. Frederick Sowrey (also Sutton's Farm) on 24th September 1916 and the **L31/LZ72** by 2nd Lt. Wulstan Tempest (North Weald) on 2nd October 1916. Lt. Alfred de Bathe Brandon (Hainault Farm) also shot down the **L33/LZ76** on 26th September 1916 and had previously assisted in downing the **L15/LZ48** on 1st April 1916.

The B.E.2c fighter was used during the period of greatest German airship activity during 1915-1916. Around 3,500 were constructed by over twenty different manufacturers. It had a length of 27ft 3in (8.31m), a height of 11ft 1½in (3.39m), a wingspan of 37ft (11.28m) and an empty weight of 1,370lb (623kg). It used a Royal Armaments Factory 1a air cooled V-8 engine with an output of 90hp (67kW). This gave a maximum speed of 72mph (116km/h) at 6,500ft (1,980m), endurance of 3hr 15min and a service ceiling of just over 10,000ft (3,050m). Climbing to 3,500ft (1,070m) took 6min 30sec and 10,000ft (3,050m) 45min 15sec resulting in a delay, if no advance warning was received, before enemy airships could be engaged.

The B.E.2c was originally armed with a .303 (7.7mm) Lewis light machine gun, for use by the observer, and could carry a bomb load of 224lb (100kg). The Lewis gun was adapted to fire upwards at a 45 degree angle, and be operated by the pilot, when the aircraft was used in a single seater night fighter role.

The B.E.2c utilised three specialist weapons that could be used in air-to-air combat against airships; Ranken darts, the French designed Le Prieur rocket and the Lewis gun with incendiary ammunition.

The Ranken dart, developed by Lieutenant-Commander Francis Ranken of the Royal Navy in 1915, consisted of a thin metal tube 9ins (23cm) long, with a cast iron pointed plug at one end, and three spring loaded arms at the other.

The arms were kept closed in the dart's dropping tube. When released, the arms opened up and locked in place to prevent the whole of the dart from entering the fabric of the airship. A small rubber stabiliser was also deployed, when the dart was released, to assist the dart to fall vertically and enter the outer skin of the airship point first.

The dart contained high explosive, black powder and phosphorus which ignited when the dart penetrated the outer skin of the airship. This was achieved by the rear of the dart being arrested by the spring loaded arms allowing the momentum of the lower section to actuate a striker and ignite the contents of the dart.

The darts, supplied in packs of 24, could be deployed individually or all at once. They were dropped from a height of up to 700ft (213m), above the airship but between 300ft (92m) and 400ft (122m) was considered the optimum altitude. If the dart was dropped too close to the airship the deceleration could be insufficient to actuate the striker. The Rankin Dart first entered service in February 1916.

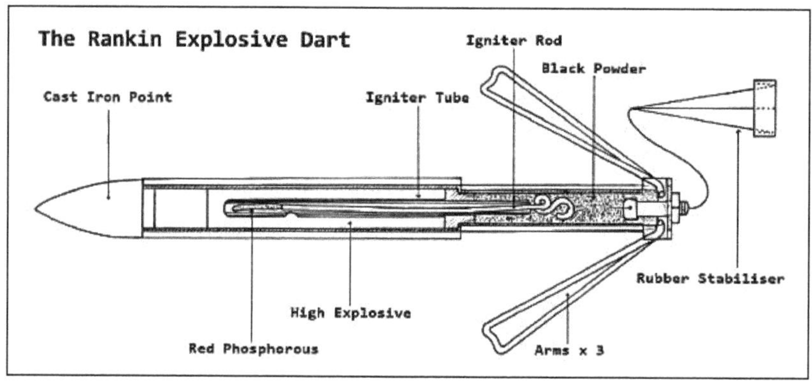

Fig 21. *A sectional drawing of the Rankin Dart showing the main components*

The Le Prieur rocket, designed by French Lieutenant Yves Le Prieur, was the precursor of the modern air-to-air missile. It was similar in appearance and function to a modern rocket firework.

The body of the rocket consisted of a cardboard tube, filled with 7oz (200g) of black powder, and was around 22in (56cm) long and 3in (7.6cm) in diameter with a conical wooden plug at the top to improve the aerodynamic properties of the rocket. This wooden cone had a triangular knife blade inserted into it, to provide a spear point, to allow the rocket to penetrate the outer skin of the airship rather than bounce off. The body of the rocket was attached to a thin, square section wooden stick, typically made of pine, which was up to 8ft (2.4m) long to provide stability in flight. The sticks were inserted in metal launch tubes, usually four per side, attached to the wing struts of the aircraft and fired electrically by the pilot. This arrangement was potentially quite dangerous if, for example, the rocket didn't clear the tube but the fuze ignited the main charge.

The rockets could only be used at short range, typically up to 126yds (115m), due to their inherent inaccuracy. This could be improved if a dive angle of 45 degrees was used when launching the rockets.

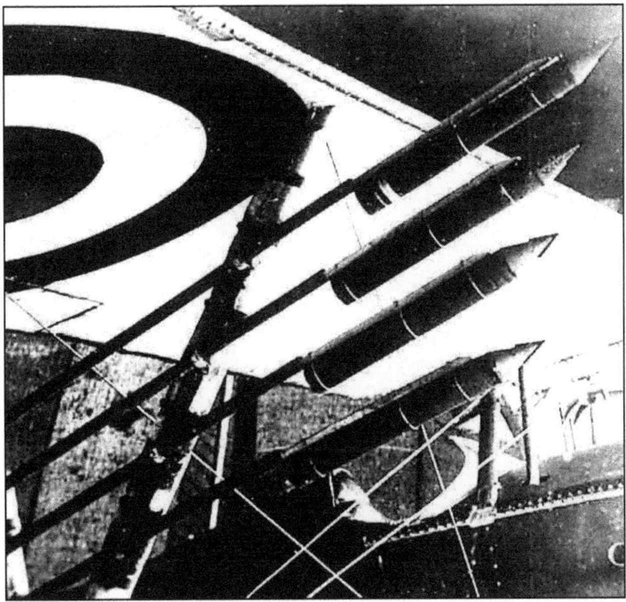

Fig 22. ***Le Prieur rockets attached to a plane***

Note the similarity to modern firework rockets.

Both the Rankin dart and the Le Prieur rocket had inherent disadvantages. They required the British pilots to fly above the enemy airship prior to deployment and had to be used at relatively close range but were still fairly inaccurate.

Despite the courage and skill of the British pilots neither weapon was particularly successful against airships, with no confirmed kills, although the Le Prieur rocket enjoyed some success against balloons in the trenches. Possibly the most famous deployment of a Rankin dart was by Lt. Alfred de Bathe Brandon, against the **L15/LZ48** on 1st April 1916, although it was never confirmed that this finally brought the airship down after it had already been hit by Ack-Ack fire.

Fortunately, a simple solution was at hand. Although full of highly flammable hydrogen gas, airships were notoriously difficult to shoot down with ordinary jacketed bullets. These passed straight through the skin without igniting the gas. It was realised that incendiary and explosive bullets could provide the solution.

Two explosive .303in (7.7mm) bullets were developed respectively by New Zealand engineer John Pomeroy and Flight Lieutenant (later Wing Commander RAF) F. A. Brock RNVR, a member of the famous fireworks family. An incendiary 'Buckingham' bullet, invented by Coventry engineer John Buckingham, was also developed at the same time. This used burning phosphorous, ignited by the propellant in the cartridge, to leave a trail of smoke, effectively the first tracer round, to provide visual confirmation of where the firer's bullets were striking. The new ammunition entered service in the second half of 1916 making the Rankin dart redundant although the Le Prieur rocket lingered on until 1918 for uses other than attacking airships.

The new explosive and incendiary rounds were often used in combination to great effect. An early success was the shooting down of the **SL11** by Lieutenant William Leefe Robinson in September 1916.

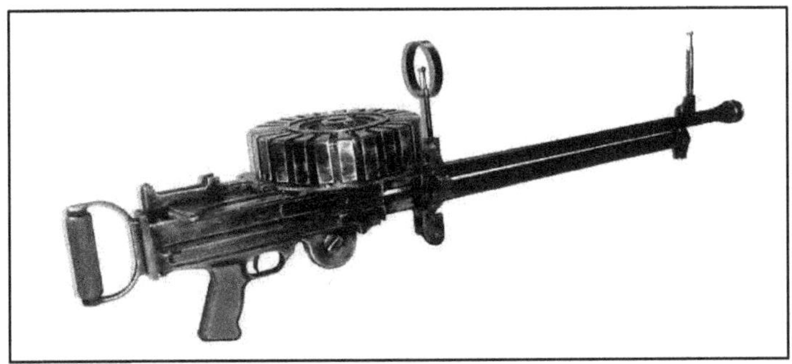

Fig 23. *The Lewis Gun in aircraft configuration*

For aircraft use the Lewis gun was normally fitted with a spade grip and different sights in addition to a 97 round magazine. The barrel shroud, used to reduce overheating of the barrel, was removed.

It was the success of explosive and incendiary bullets that was credited with persuading the German Army to abandon the use of airships for bombing raids against Great Britain in 1916.

THE BADGES

This is a selection of insignia worn by the main protagonists in the Zeppelin air raids on London:

Fig 24. ***German Zeppelin Pilot qualification badge***

The following British military units were involved in the defence of London against air raids:

Royal Naval Volunteer Reserve Anti-Aircraft Corps

Royal Flying Corps 19 Reserve Aircraft Squadron
Royal Flying Corps 39 (Home Defence) Squadron

Royal Garrison Artillery Cornwall
Royal Garrison Artillery Essex and Suffolk
Royal Garrison Artillery Glamorgan
Royal Garrison Artillery Kent
Royal Garrison Artillery London

Royal Artillery

London Electrical Engineers
Tyne Electrical Engineers
Royal Engineers

Army Service Corps

The Admiralty assumed responsibility for the air defences of London at the start of the Great War. The Royal Naval Volunteer Reserve Anti-Aircraft Corps was responsible fulfilling this role from 1914 until the beginning of 1915. It then became the Royal Naval Air Service Anti-Aircraft Corps. Badges were almost identical but with the initials 'RNAS AAC'.

Fig 25. ***Royal Naval Volunteer Reserve Anti-Aircraft Corps cap (left) and collar badge for dress uniform***

Fig 26. ***Royal Naval Volunteer Reserve Anti-Aircraft Corps shoulder titles metal (left) and cloth***

The War Office regained responsibility for air defence at the start of 1916 and this was undertaken by the RGA (anti-aircraft guns), RE (searchlights) and RFC (aerial combat).

Fig 27. ***Royal Garrison Artillery cap badge***

Five RGA units were primarily involved in the defence of London; Cornwall, Essex & Suffolk, Glamorgan, Kent and London.

Fig 28. ***Royal Garrison Artillery Cornwall (left) and Essex & Suffolk brass shoulder titles***

Fig 29. ***Royal Garrison Artillery Glamorgan (left) and Kent brass shoulder titles***

Fig 30. ***Royal Garrison Artillery London brass shoulder titles***

The brass shoulder badges illustrated above were worn by the territorial (TF) soldiers of the Royal Garrison Artillery in London that were manning the anti-aircraft guns side by side with the TF Royal Engineers London (Territorial) searchlight units. In 1917 The Territorial Forces (TF) were given new numbers. Number ranges were allocated to each TF unit making it possible to trace a soldier's unit if his number is known.

Fig 31. ***Royal Engineers cap badge***

Fig 32. ***Royal Engineers London (left) and Tyne brass shoulder title***

The Royal Engineers had brass shoulder titles of simply RE but the Electrical Engineers on the searchlights had brass shoulder badges showing T/RE/LONDON or T/RE/TYNE. These were the brass shoulder title worn by the Territorial Royal Engineers that manned the searchlights during 1914-15 in London. The Territorial Force (TF) was renamed to The Territorial Army (TA) on 1st October 1920.

Fig 33. ***Royal Flying Corps cap badge***

Fig 34. ***Royal Flying Corps Pilot's Wing***

Fig 35. ***Royal Flying Corps cloth shoulder title***

Fig 36. ***Royal Flying Corps brass (left) and bullion shoulder titles***

Fig 37. ***Army Service Corps brass cap badge***

Fig 38. ***Army Service Corps brass shoulder titles (L-R) Territorial, ASC and Mechanical Transport***

THE SOUVENIRS

Despite the public concern created by the raids there was a good demand for Zeppelin souvenirs. The crested china companies at the time produced, within days of memorable events, very accurate white porcelain mementoes of aeroplanes, Zeppelins and Zeppelin bombs.

The range of First World War crested china items produced was very large and would fill a book of its own; there are tanks, guns, searchlights, aircraft, airships, bombs, shells, bullets, ships, submarines, famous figures and memorials.

Zeppelin bombs were wrapped in flammable material of rope that had been soaked in tar. They had handles as they were dropped by hand. These china mementoes were manufactured and were on sale within days of the bombs being dropped from the Zeppelins.

Fig 39. ***Crested china model of the L33/LZ76***

The **L33/LZ76** was shot down by Lieutenant Alfred de Bathe Brandon on 23rd September 1916.

The following example is a model of an incendiary bomb that was dropped on Putney in London. It is 3 in (7.5cm) high and was made by Carlton China of Stoke on Trent.

Fig 40. ***Crested china model of an incendiary bomb bearing the crest of Putney in London***

Illustrated below is a model of a different type of bomb dropped on Skegness by a Zeppelin. It is 3.2in (8cm) high and was made by the Arcadian China Co. It was retailed by a hairdresser in Skegness named E.G. Sayer.

Fig 41. ***Crested china model of an incendiary bomb bearing the crest of Skegness in Lincolnshire***

The ribbed effect represents the rope wrapped around the bomb. The rope was impregnated with tar to create fires.

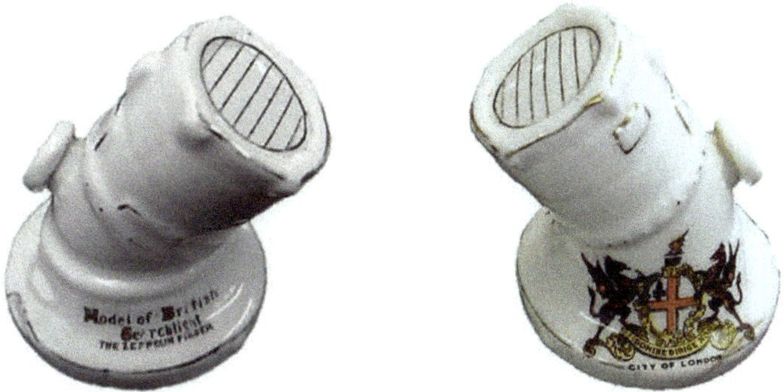

Fig 42. ***'The Zeppelin Finder'. Crested china model of a searchlight***

Fig 43. ***Two examples of crested china fighters.***

Fig 44. ***A souvenir badge created from a piece of the wreckage from the L15/LZ48***

PART 2 - ZEPPELIN L15 & THE WAKEFIELD GOLD MEDAL

Fig 45. ***The Sir Charles Wakefield Gold Medal***

SIR CHARLES WAKEFIELD

Lord Wakefield (then Colonel Sir Charles Cheers Wakefield) was the Lord Mayor of London 1915-1916 during the Great War.

He was very supportive of the military during this period and visited the Front Line. He was founder and governing director of Wakefield Oil which became the Castrol Oil Company.

An inventor, businessman, philanthropist and patriot, he was raised to the peerage as Baron Wakefield of Hythe in 1930 before being made Viscount Wakefield of Hythe in 1934. He died in 1941.

Fig 46. ***Sir Charles Wakefield***

Following increasing public dismay, at the continuing Zeppelin bombing raids, The Lord Mayor had offered a prize of £500 to the first person to shoot down a Zeppelin over London. The nominal number of crew on an anti-aircraft gun was eleven. That would have given each gunner £45.9s.1d. It would have been less if he included the searchlight teams as I have discovered there were Royal Engineers on the Darenth and Woolwich searchlights who received the medals.

It was Captain Joseph Harris who first claimed the reward from Sir Charles Wakefield. He was in command of the TRGA anti-aircraft guns at Purfleet near Thurrock to the east of London. On the 3rd

April 1916 he wrote to the Lord Mayor of London claiming the £500 prize on behalf of his gun crew. The War Office ruled that an army unit was not allowed to accept such an award for doing what was effectively its job. This was in direct contrast to Lt. Leefe Robinson of the Royal Flying Corps who received his Victoria Cross and reward of £3,500 later that same year for shooting down the Shutte-Lanz airship **SL11**. To give you an idea of the value of this prize money the White Hart Hotel in Honiton, Devon sold for £2,000 in 1917. The War Office eventually decided that the action was a joint effort by all the RGA anti-aircraft guns in the area of the Thames Estuary and they should all share the Lord Mayor's reward.

The Royal Garrison Artillery manned the guns and the Royal Engineers owned and operated the searchlights at Purfleet, Dartford, Woolwich, Hilly Fields, Putney, Wembley and Waltham. As there were a total of 353 personnel involved that would have worked out at £1.8s.3¾d each. The strange thing was that the authorities refused to award any military decorations to the ground troops for this auspicious event.

THE WAKEFIELD GOLD MEDAL

As the War Office had decreed that no one individual could claim the £500 cash prize, and a number of gun crews claimed to have brought the **L15/LZ48** down, Sir Charles Wakefield personally designed and paid for a 9 carat (9.375) gold medal to be awarded to all the gun crews that he felt were involved. These were struck and hallmarked in Birmingham. The medals were 1 $^{9}/_{64}$ inches (29mm) in diameter and $^{1}/_{16}$ inch (1.5mm) thick. They weighed 1oz.

Fig 47. ***The hallmark on the reverse of the medal. From left to right this reads; 9 Carat, .375 gold content, Birmingham and 1916***

The medals were intended to be commemorative, rather than for wear, but many were subsequently converted by the addition of a hanger for a ribbon.

Fig 48. ***An example of an ornate hanger added to the medal to allow it to be worn***

Some were just a simple loop of gold wire soldered to the medal.

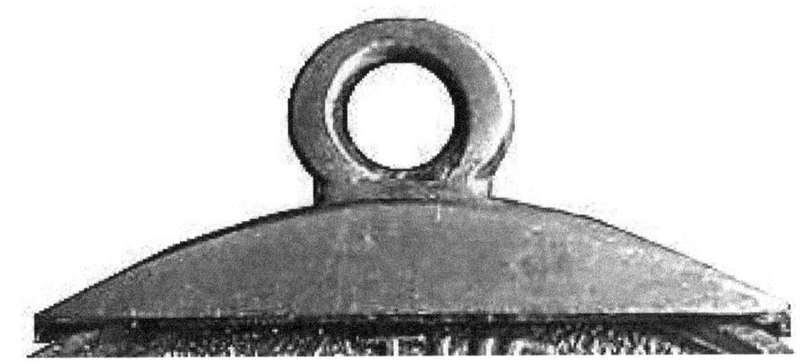

Fig 49. ***An example of a more substantial loop hanger***

The medals were enclosed in fine red leather cases with silk lining embossed with the name of the manufacturer Mappin & Webb Ltd. of 2, Queen Victoria Street, London. E.C.

The obverse of the medal is inscribed 'PRESENTED BY THE LORD MAYOR COLONEL SIR CHARLES WAKEFIELD' and features the Wakefield coat of arms with the motto 'VIGILANS ET AUDAX' or 'Vigilant and Bold'. The Reverse of the medal is very attractive with an illustration of the type of gun used to bring the **L15/LZ48** down. This appears to be the 1916 QF 3 in. 20 cwt. gun designed by Vickers. It fired a 16 pound (7.26 kg) shell with a muzzle velocity of 2,000fps (609m/sec) to a maximum height of 22,000ft (6,705m). The type 80b time and percussion fuze was used. Ironically, this fuze was invented by the German armaments company Krupp.

The reverse of the medal, as well as bearing the Birmingham hallmark and the M&W back stamp, is also inscribed with the recipient's name and rank and the words, 'L15' and 'WELL HIT MARCH 31ST – 1ST APRIL 1916'.

The representation of the recipient's rank was dependent on the length of their initials (if present) and surname rather than the use of a standard format. This resulted in the use of both 'GUNNER' and 'GUNR'. There are at least two recorded instances, Lieutenant G. Greenway and Gunner Charles Dunston, where names were incorrectly inscribed on the medals. Lieutenant Greenway was recorded as 'Greenaway' and Gunner Dunston as 'Dunstan'. This may imply that the medal roll was handwritten, rather than typed, as experienced engravers do not make many mistakes as these can be very costly.

As there is currently no known copy of the medal roll in existence, military collectors appear to have ignored them as military awards classing them with sport awards, plaques and medallions. I have spoken with three owners of Wakefield medals who sold them as they were unable to discover any useful information concerning the award. It is possible that a number of these medals have been melted down for their scrap value in the last few years but a number have been preserved by the recipients' families, museums and private collectors. The medal belonging to Captain Joseph Harris, who was the first claimant of the Wakefield Prize and later went on to become a Lt. Colonel in the Royal Artillery, is owned by his grandson Peter Harris. The medal warded to Gunner Richard James (Jim) Richards is owned by his family in the USA and Gunner R. Evans' Medal is in the Southend-on-Sea Museum.

The medal illustrated below was awarded to Gunner Hollow of the Royal Garrison Artillery. He was a member of the Territorial Royal Garrison Artillery and lived in London. I have been unable to discover any other details regarding this recipient.

Fig 50. ***The Sir Charles Wakefield Gold Medal manufactured by Mappin & Webb Ltd. Obverse***

Fig 51. ***The Sir Charles Wakefield Gold Medal, reverse, showing gun and recipient's name***

Researching medal recipients can be a challenge as the award was not recorded on their military record.

Fig 52. ***Details of the leather presentation box***

Fig 53. ***Wakefield Gold Medal to Gunner Hollow***

The original leather presentation box shows Mappin & Webb's London address

THE AWARD OF THE MEDALS

I have found it difficult to understand why there appears to be no official record of this extraordinary event and a list of the recipients, which was required for the engraving of the medals, kept for posterity.

One possible explanation is that the War Office, despite the potential for boosting the morale of the civilian population, displayed ambivalence towards Sir Charles Wakefield's award which was considered to have been made in a private capacity. Captain Joseph Harris was disqualified by the War Office from claiming the original £500 prize on behalf of his gun crew.

Fig 54. ***Some of the Gunners who shot down the L15/LZ48***

When it was decided to produce and award gold medals instead there was no evidence of a grand parade which would have been immensely popular with war-weary Londoners who had suffered nightly as a result of the Zeppelin raids. I have researched Sir Charles Wakefield's official journal, as Lord Mayor, and there is no mention of an awards ceremony during his year in office. The only reference to Zeppelins occurs on 25th September 1916. This states "Lord Mayor opens an exhibition of Zeppelin relics at the Armoury House, Finsbury, in aid of the Kitchener Memorial Fund and the City branch of the British Red Cross".

This appears to confirm that the award of the medals was a personal gesture by Sir Charles Wakefield, with tacit approval from the War Office, and was not made in his official capacity as Lord Mayor of London.

Despite extensive research I have only discovered three references relating to the award of the medals. The first is on page 248 of 'The Commercial Motor' from November 16th 1916. This states that Sir Charles Wakefield handed over 'some 350 gold medals' to GHQ Home Forces at The Horse Guards S.W. a few days before completing his year of office as Lord Mayor of London.

These were presumably passed on to the individuals concerned at a small parade at each individual gun or searchlight emplacement. Recipients were advised that the medals, which were not recorded on the medal card of their army records, could not be worn on uniform. Indeed they had no means of attaching a ribbon but a number of recipients had hangers of different designs, plain or decorative, added afterward to allow them to be worn on civilian dress with their official war medals.

Gold Medals from Sir C. C. Wakefield.

Sir Charles Cheers Wakefield, a few days before completing his year of office as Lord Mayor of London, handed over to General Headquarters of Home Forces, at the Horse Guards, S.W., some 350 gold medals for distribution to officers and men who shared the responsibility for bringing down Zeppelin "L15" at the end of March last, in the Thames Estuary. This was the only course for Sir C. C. Wakefield, with official approval, to adopt in discharge of his promise to give £500 to the first person or persons who brought down a Zeppelin in Great Britain.

Fig 55. *Extract from 'The Commercial Motor' dated November 16th 1916*

Note the terms 'handed over' and 'distribution' implying this was not done at a single formal parade.

The second, more comprehensive, reference I discovered was an article in the Royal United

Services Institute (RUSI) Journal Volume 95, Issue 759, of August 1950. This is entitled *The Destruction of Zeppelin L.15 – An early A.A. Success* and was written by Brigadier H.B. Latham. The article is a useful source of reference, as it was written by a senior officer, and was produced only thirty or so years after the Zeppelin raids meaning that many of the participants in the downing of the L15 were still alive. This does not mean that the information in the article is unimpeachable but it does originate from a highly respected source. The most useful information contained in the article is as follows:

1) It was the G.O.C.-in-C. Home Forces, Field-Marshall Lord French, who, despite commending a number of the A.A. gun crews, took the decision that no serving member of the armed forces should receive a cash reward for shooting down the L15 which he considered to be their duty. It was therefore suggested to Sir Charles Wakefield, who had submitted Captain Joseph Harris' claim for the prize to the War Office for approval, that the money should be spent on gold medals instead.
2) Medal Rolls were prepared and submitted to the War Office by the units concerned.
3) 353 gold medals were produced by Mappin & Webb and 'issued' in November 1916 immediately prior to Sir Charles Wakefield leaving office.

4) The gun reproduced on the reverse of the medal is reported to be the 3 in. 20 cwt. variant.
5) The medal was intended to be a keepsake and not worn although many were adapted, by the addition of a hanger, to facilitate this.
6) Only 8 of the 27 guns, defending London and the Thames area, were cited for the award of medals. The locations, gun type(s) and associated units were as follows:
   - Dartford. 1 x 3 in. 20 cwt. 5 Coy. Cornwall R.G.A. (T.A.)
   - Purfleet. 1 x 3 in. 20 cwt. & 2 x pom-poms. 3 Coy. Essex and Suffolk R.G.A. (T.A.)
   - Erith. 2 x 6 pdrs. 5 Coy. Cornwall R.G.A. (T.A.)
   - Abbey Wood. 2 x 3 in. 20 cwt. Regular R.A.
   - Southern Outfall.1 x 3 in. 20 cwt & 1 x 13 pdr. 2 Coy. Glamorgan R.G.A. (T.A.)
   - Plumstead Common. 1 x 3 in. 20 cwt. & 1 x 13 pdr. 2 Coy. Glamorgan R.G.A. (T.A.)
   - Royal Arsenal Defences.1 x 3 in. 5 cwt., 2 x 6 pdrs & 1 x pom-pom. Regular R.A. and Kent R.G.A. (T.A.)
   - North Woolwich.1 x 3 in. 5 cwt. Regular R.A.
7) During the Great War, 72 raids were made on the British mainland, killing 833 persons, injuring 2,002, and causing more than two million pounds worth of damage.
8) All the searchlights were manned by the London Electrical Engineers, R.E. (T.A.), with

the exception of the one sited at Darenth which was manned by a detachment of the Tyne Electrical Engineers, R.E. (T.A.).

The third and most exciting reference is a page from the diary of 118523 Gunner Edward John Eddy of the Cornwall RGA. Gunner Eddy was born on 2nd June 1893 in Mawnan, Falmouth, Cornwall and volunteered for the RGA in 1914. Gunner Eddy was the oldest of seven brothers of whom another two served in the Great War. All three returned safely from the hostilities. He served in the air defence of London and with the British Expeditionary Force in France before being demobilised in 1919. The contents of his diary were kindly made available to me by his granddaughter Linda.

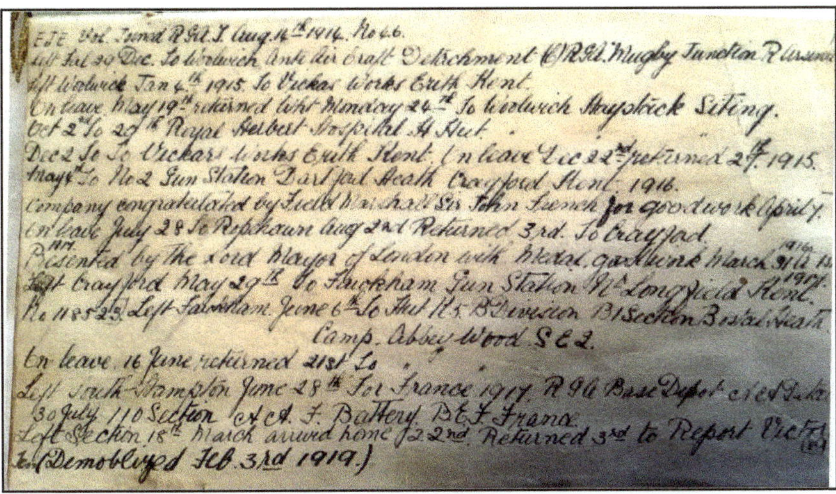

E.J.E. Vol. Joined R.G.A. T. Aug. 14th 1914. No 4.6.
Left Fal 20 Dec. To Woolwich Anti Air Craft Detachment [illegible] R.G.A. Rugby Junction [illegible]
Left Woolwich Jan 4th 1915. To Vickers Works Erith Kent.
On leave May 19th returned Whit Monday 24th To Woolwich Haystack Siting.
Oct 2nd To 29th Royal Herbert Hospital H Hut.
Dec 2 To To Vickers Works Erith Kent. On leave Dec 22nd returned 27. 1915.
May 4th To No 2 Gun Station Dartford Heath Crayford Kent. 1916.
Company congratulated by Field Marshall Sir John French for good work April 7.
On leave July 28 To Redruth Aug 2nd Returned 3rd. To Crayford.
Presented by the Lord Mayor of London with Medal, good work March 31st 1916
Left Crayford May 29th To Faversham Gun Station Nr Longfield Kent. 1917.
No 118523 Left Faversham June 6th To Hut H5 B Division B1 Section Bostal Heath
Camp. Abbey Wood S.E.2.
On leave 16 June returned 21st To
Left South Hampton June 28th For France 1917. R.G.A. Base Depot [illegible]
30 July 110 Section A.A. F. Battery B.E.F. France.
Left Section 18th March arrived home Feb 22nd. Returned 3rd to Report [illegible]
(Demoblized Feb. 3rd 1919.)

Fig 56. *Extract from the diary of 118523 Gunner Edward John Eddy*

The following is a transcript of this page:

EJE Vol. joined RGA.T. Aug. 14th 1914. No 46.

Left Fal 29 Dec. to Woolwich Anti Air Craft Detachment (C) RGA. Mugby Junction R Arsenal.

Left Woolwich Jan 4th 1915. to Vickers Works Erith Kent.

On leave. May 19th returned Wht Monday 24th to Woolwich Haystack siting.

Oct 2nd to 29th Royal Herbert Hospital H Hut.

Dec 2nd to to [sic] Vickers Works Erith Kent. On leave Dec 22nd returned 27th 1915.

May 4th to No 2 Gun Station Dartford Heath Crayford Kent. 1916.

Company congratulated by Field Marshall [sic] Sir John French for good work April 7.

On leave July 28 to Ropehawn Aug 2nd returned 3rd to Crayford.

1917 1916

Presented by the Lord Mayor of London with medal, good work March 31st A 1st.

1917

Left Crayford May 29th to Fawkham Gun Station near Longfield Kent.

No 118523 left Fawkham June 6th to hut H5 B Division. B1 section Bostal [sic] Heath

Camp. Abbey Wood SE2.

On leave 16th June returned 21st June to " "

Left Southampton June 28th for France 1917 RGA Base Depot AA detail.

30th July 110 section AA F. Battery BEF France 1917.

Left section 18th March arrived home 22nd. Returned 3rd to report Victoria April 4th 1918.

Then [?] (Demoblised [sic] Feb 3rd 1919.)

Fig 57. ***A transcription of the diary page of 118523 Gunner Edward John Eddy***

This historically important document is possibly the only currently known account of the medal presentation by one of the recipients and contains some excellent supplementary information.

Two events are of particular interest. The first is a visit by Field-Marshal Lord French, G.O.C.-in-C. Home Forces, on April 7th 1916 to congratulate the gun crew on their good work following the downing of the L15/LZ48 on the night of 31st March. The visit appears to have taken place at the Vickers Works in Erith shortly before the gun crew relocated to No. 2 Gun Station, Dartford Heath near Crayford on 4th May 1916.

The second and most interesting event, without doubt, is a visit by Sir Charles Wakefield on 1st April 1917 to Dartford Heath near Crayford to present the gun crew with their gold medals in person. Gunner Eddy's diary states:

"1917 Presented by the Lord Mayor of London with medal, good work March 31st 1916 A 1st. 1917"

It is not clear if this was a single gesture by Sir Charles Wakefield, who had left office the previous November, or whether he personally presented all gun and searchlight crews, awarded the medal, in this manner. It is possible that some crews were presented with their medals by their Officer Commanding. Brigadier Latham, in his RUSI paper, uses the term 'issued', in relation to the medals, but this may be synonymous to the term 'handed over' (to the War Office) used in *The Commercial Motor*. What is incontrovertible, however, is that Sir Charles Wakefield did personally present medals to at least one gun crew after he left office. Although the medals were a private gesture, this would certainly account for the absence of any mention of medal presentations by Sir Charles in his official journal whilst in office.

There are some interesting insights into service in the RGA in Gunner Eddy's notes. It is generally accepted that 5 Coy, Cornwall RGA was deployed at Dartford and Erith but Gunner Eddy also mentions Woolwich AA Detachment (C) RGA, Mugby Junction Royal Arsenal. This is an interesting reference as Mugby Junction is the name of a collection of railway related short stories written by Charles Dickens and a small number of collaborative authors. In the context used by Gunner Eddy, Mugby Junction is an area within the Royal Arsenal at Woolwich.

This 'city within a city' covered almost three square miles and was vital to the defence of Great Britain and her Empire as it was used to develop and test munitions particularly artillery shells.

The Royal Arsenal started to decline in the 1920s, and, despite a reprieve in WWII, was finally closed in the mid-1960s. It has now been redeveloped for housing and business use but back in the Great

War it was at its zenith and a prime target for Zeppelin bombs. The Arsenal contained one of the densest private rail networks in Great Britain, if not the world, with over 140 miles of standard and narrow gauge track, for the movement of staff and munitions, crammed into little over two square miles. A particular junction was named 'Mugby Junction' after the Dickens book.

Fig 58. ***A narrow gauge locomotive with a passenger train within the Royal Arsenal railway system***

Mention is also made in Gunner Eddy's diary of 'Woolwich Haystack Siting'. Although it is not possible to identify the exact location of this today, parts of Woolwich, including the more remote areas of the Royal Arsenal, were semi-rural in the Great War and groups of haystacks were a common sight.

This entry almost certainly refers to one such location.

Gunner Eddy spent 27 days, from 2nd - 29th October 1915, in H Hut at the Royal Herbert Hospital in Greenwich. It is unclear whether this was as the result of a medical condition or the gun crew was billeted there temporarily. The buildings of the former hospital, which finally closed in 1977, survive as luxury apartments.

Fig 59. ***The Royal Herbert Hospital, Greenwich***

During 1917, Gunner Eddy was stationed at two other nearby locations, Fawkham Gun Station near Longfield in Kent and Bostall Heath in Abbey Wood, SE2.

Despite the seriousness of the war, soldiers were usually permitted leave. This was normally allocated in blocks of five days at a time. Gunner Eddy took four periods of leave between 1915 and 1917 including Christmas 1915 and visiting Cornwall in July 1916.

In conclusion, it is hard to escape the feeling that the War Office regarded Sir Charles Wakefield's prize as a distraction and were a reluctant participant in the proceedings.

In contrast, by having the medals struck and handing these over before leaving office, Sir Charles honourably discharged his commitment to a £500 prize for the shooting down of the first Zeppelin.

A SUMMARY FOR THE 353 GOLD MEDALS AWARDED

One of the greatest challenges facing military historians, in the absence of a definitive medal roll, is that it is difficult to get the figures to add up. *The Commercial Motor* stated 'some 350 gold medals' were distributed and this is corroborated by Brigadier H. B. Latham, in his RUSI article, which suggests the number was 353. The very precise figure given may indicate possession of, or access to, the medal roll but there is no means, almost seventy years later, of verifying this.

I have attempted to extrapolate the total number of medals awarded as follows:

There were twelve Searchlights in London but I believe only two were awarded medals; the Woolwich Searchlight, which was the first to light up the **L15/LZ48** Zeppelin, and the Darenth Searchlight at Dartford, Kent which picked out the **L15/LZ48** as it descended and tried to escape towards the sea.

At that time there were twenty-seven anti-aircraft guns in London. There were ancillary personnel attached to the guns and searchlights and at least two ASC drivers and a member of the RFC received the Wakefield Medal. Without the medal roll I have therefore made the following assumptions to supplement my research.

If each of the twenty-seven anti-aircraft guns in London had a nominal crew of eleven comprising one Officer and ten Other Ranks this equals a total of two hundred and ninety-seven men for the guns. This of course ignores Brigadier Latham's statement, in his RUSI paper, that only eight of the twenty-seven guns were cited, as a result of the action, although there were multiple guns at some locations that would increase the total. Unless all guns were included it would be very difficult to reach a total of 353 medals.

There were also nominally ten men on the Woolwich Searchlight and another ten on the Darenth

Searchlight, which illuminated the **L15/LZ48**, giving a total of three hundred and seventeen. We also know for certain that two ASC drivers, attached to searchlights, and 2nd Lt. Alfred de Bathe Brandon of the RFC received the Wakefield Medal which gives a grand total of three hundred and twenty.

This leaves thirty-three medals still unaccounted for if Brigadier Latham's figure is correct. Had medals been awarded to all the RE searchlight crews, the total medals would have comfortably exceeded the stated total of 353. I therefore believe it likely that the remainder of the medals, currently unaccounted for, were awarded to other personnel attached to the guns or searchlights.

There is no doubt that, in the continuing absence of a definitive medal roll, the list of recipients will continue to generate research and debate for many years to come.

Fig 60. ***A portrait of Zeppelin L15/LZ48***

Fig 61. ***A postcard showing the wreckage of the L15/LZ48 in the English Channel***

RECIPIENTS OF THE SIR CHARLES WAKEFIELD GOLD MEDAL

The following, still incomplete, list of recipients of the Wakefield Medal, by Corps or Regiment, has been compiled from a number of sources. These include books, newspapers, magazines, the Internet, military archives, auctions, and museums. The excellent list created by R. J. Sirley for his 1982 article in *Medal News* has been invaluable for cross checking recipients' names.

The following is a list of recipients by rank within unit. It contains some duplicate names but these may refer to members of the same family and additional research is required. An alphabetical list of the recipients, with additional information, is reproduced at Appendix 1.

LIST OF MEDAL RECIPIENTS BY UNIT AND RANK

2 Company Glamorgan RGA (TF)

Captain	Gunning-Carr	A
Lieutenant	Barnett	R N
Lieutenant	Greenway	G
Lieutenant	Pring	W I
Lieutenant	Walker	J
BSM	Harper	
CQMS	Grumbridge	G
Sergeant	Avery	A
Sergeant	Brock	E
Sergeant	Holmes	W
Sergeant	Stocker	S
Bombardier	Bird	H
Bombardier	Viggers	A
Bombardier	Ward	W
Bombardier	Wyatt	C
Corporal	Affley	T
Corporal	Creemer	F
Corporal	Elliott	E
Corporal	Evans	H W
Gunner	Anderson	
Gunner	Barnes	
Gunner	Barry	H
Gunner	Berrill	W
Gunner	Boshier	A
Gunner	Bowen	J

Gunner	Brewer	A
Gunner	Broomfield	C
Gunner	Callaghan	E
Gunner	Chidgey	
Gunner	Coggins	G
Gunner	Cope	W
Gunner	Cox	J
Gunner	Crimmings	D
Gunner	Curtis	E
Gunner	Curtis	W J
Gunner	Donaghue	
Gunner	Dunscombe	A
Gunner	Essex	J
Gunner	Evans	D
Gunner	Evans	F
Gunner	Gabb	I
Gunner	Gomer	P
Gunner	Gough	T
Gunner	Gronow	P
Gunner	Haines	
Gunner	Hancock	G
Gunner	Harvey	
Gunner	Hill	F
Gunner	Hinksman	W H
Gunner	Hooper	G
Gunner	Hope	T
Gunner	John	L
Gunner	Jones	E
Gunner	Jones	W

Gunner	Lewis	C T B
Gunner	Lewis	E
Gunner	March	C
Gunner	Marfell	T
Gunner	May	W
Gunner	McDonald	
Gunner	McDonald	
Gunner	Morgan	
Gunner	Munro	A
Gunner	Nichols	J
Gunner	Oakley	W
Gunner	Page	G
Gunner	Page	W
Gunner	Parkhouse	W
Gunner	Peach	E
Gunner	Pope	T
Gunner	Richards	Richard James
Gunner	Tarr	H
Gunner	Thomas	H
Gunner	Thompson	J H
Gunner	Troak	E
Gunner	Tucker	T
Gunner	Tucker	W
Gunner	Vigar	P
Gunner	White	H
Gunner	Williamson	W
Trumpeter	Ball	F
Trumpeter	Lewis	W

3 Company Essex and Suffolk RGA (TF)

Captain	Harris	Joseph
Lieutenant	Fox	
Lieutenant	Howerd	L G
Lieutenant	Laird	
Lieutenant	Newton	
RQMS	Joscelyne	F
Sergeant	French	
Sergeant	Guiver	V
Bombardier	Dawkins	
Bombardier	Phillips	William
Corporal	Beale	
Corporal	Dorkins	G M
Corporal	Downer	
Gunner	Atwood	
Gunner	Birrell	
Gunner	Birrell	
Gunner	Clarke	
Gunner	Cogger	S
Gunner	Dawkins	
Gunner	Derbyshire	
Gunner	Dorkins	Reginald L
Gunner	Edwards	
Gunner	Evans	
Gunner	Fish	
Gunner	Flack	
Gunner	Gladwell	Arthur Charles
Gunner	Gladwin	

Gunner	Goddard	
Gunner	Goodard	
Gunner	Green	
Gunner	Holland	
Gunner	Hooper	
Gunner	Horsley	
Gunner	Kidd	
Gunner	King	
Gunner	Langdon	
Gunner	Lazell	
Gunner	Lewis	
Gunner	Livermore	
Gunner	Moore	
Gunner	Nethercote	Walter Harold
Gunner	Reynolds	T
Gunner	Ridd	J
Gunner	Sayers	
Gunner	Shelley	
Gunner	Sullivan	
Gunner	Tubbs	Walter Dean
Gunner	Warren	

5 Company Cornwall RGA (TF)

Lieutenant	Moffat	
2 Lieutenant	Causer	D S
2 Lieutenant	Dudgeon	
2 Lieutenant	Stokes	J W G
Sergeant	Richards	
Sergeant	Rutter	H T

Bombardier	Dave	
Bombardier	Hodge	S
Bombardier	James	S
Bombardier	Tregears	
Gunner	Allen	J
Gunner	Allen	S
Gunner	Berryman	J
Gunner	Bishop	
Gunner	Carthew	T
Gunner	Cocking	
Gunner	Cothey	J
Gunner	Couch	R
Gunner	Delve	C
Gunner	Dunston	Charles
Gunner	Eddy	Edward John
Gunner	Freeman	
Gunner	Geach	W
Gunner	Gilbert	F
Gunner	Harris	W
Gunner	Harris	
Gunner	Hill	T
Gunner	James	
Gunner	Jose	R
Gunner	Lugg	
Gunner	Martin	
Gunner	Mildren	W H
Gunner	Panlis	R
Gunner	Panlis	W
Gunner	Paynter	

Gunner	Rolling	Stanley C
Gunner	Sampson	E
Gunner	Semmens	W
Gunner	Smith	F H
Gunner	Sowden	
Gunner	Stool	S
Gunner	Thomas	
Gunner	Williams	T
Gunner	Woolcock	W

6 Company London Electrical Engineers RE (TF)

Captain	Hunter	E B
Staff Sergeant	Howard	P H
Corporal	Guest	W A
Sapper	Cushway	A J
Sapper	Rouse	J H
Sapper	Taylor	

9 Company Tyne Electrical Engineers RE (TF)

Sergeant	Donaldson	J
Corporal	Bolt	P
L/Corporal	Armstrong	S
Sapper	Allan	F
Sapper	Elliott	R
Sapper	Hastings	L
Sapper	King	John J
Sapper	Milburn	W
Sapper	Williams	W
Sapper	Williamson	W

Kent RGA (TF)

Captain	Pearce	F D
Lieutenant	Wilson	R

Regulars and "K" Army RA

Lieutenant	Ingram	
Sergeant	Arthur	A
Bombardier	Sargent	A
Gunner	Ireland	
Gunner	Julien	F
Gunner	Lewis	
Gunner	Nosegood	
Gunner	Riley	
Gunner	Sirley	B
Gunner	Turner	

Army Service Corps

Driver	Colman	Oliver John
Driver	Rose	H J J

Royal Engineers

Sapper	Earl	H M
Sapper	Hammant	Walter R
Sapper	Hogan	Frank Thomas
Sapper	Hogan	J
Sapper	McCann	
Sapper	Parker	J F

Royal Flying Corps 19 RA Squadron

2 Lieutenant	de Bath Brandon	Alfred

Royal Garrison Artillery NFDK

Lieutenant	Hodgins	Arthur Wilfred Marrable
Sergeant	Bicheno	Charles
Bombardier	Shawcross	Herbert
Corporal	Penfold	H J
Gunner	Dargan	F
Gunner	Hancock	Clifford
Gunner	Hollow	
Gunner	Ireland	Alfred
Gunner	Pearce	Alfred J

Unknown Corps or Regiment

Lieutenant	Smith	
Sergeant	Cooper	George H
Bombardier	Callaghan	R
Corporal	Brown	C
Gunner	Berrill	W
Gunner	Birch	Harry
Gunner	Butler	
Gunner	Cox	
Gunner	Drew	Arthur Edward
Gunner	Evans	R
Gunner	Fry	
Gunner	Hearing	Robert H

Gunner	Hosegood	
Gunner	Merrifield	
Gunner	Morgan	
Gunner	Murray	
Gunner	O'Keefe	
Gunner	Prescott	Thomas
Gunner	Sykes	H
Gunner	Taylor	Frank Charles
Gunner	Young	J
Gunner	Hesketh	
Private	Scrase	F W
	Allaway	Sidney Alfred

There are still over 100 medals unaccounted for. These were almost certainly allocated between the RGA (TF), RA, RE (Searchlights) and ASC. I believe the Engineers on the above list were on the Woolwich and Darenth searchlights.

It was the Woolwich searchlight that illuminated the L15 for the first time. Listed below are the men that were on the Darenth searchlight detachment. They were part of the No. 9 Tyne Mobile Searchlight Company:

Sgt J. Donaldson RE	Sapper. A.L. Hastings RE
Cpl. P. Bolt RE	Sapper. J. King RE
L/Cpl. S. Armstrong RE	Sapper. W. Milburn RE
Sapper. F. Allan RE	Sapper. W. Williams RE
Sapper. R. Elliot RE	Sapper. W. Williamson RE

2nd Lt. Alfred de Bathe Brandon RFC, who was awarded the Military Cross for his actions after attacking the L15, also received the Wakefield Medal. This was not reported as widely as it might have been.

One can understand the reasons for this as 2nd Lt. Brandon attacked the Zeppelin as it was retreating towards the sea after having its gas bags ruptured by the London based Territorial Royal Garrison Artillery.

The incident was to generate controversy sixteen years later when the Commander of the L15 Kapitänleutnant Joachim Breithaupt, who was taken prisoner at the time, gave a radio lecture that was chronicled in the BBC publication *The Listener* of 8th June 1932. In this, he stated that it was ground anti-aircraft fire that damaged the L15, causing it to crash, rather than any intervention by Lt. Brandon.

Brandon, who had returned to his native New Zealand to practice law following the Great War, was forced to defend his position against possible allegations that he had accepted an MC under false pretences. This defence included testimony from some of the captured officers from the L15 stating that "The airman had got them".

Alfred de Bathe Brandon MC DSO MID passed away in 1974 aged 90 years.

Fig 62. ***Captain Joachim Breithaupt on board the L15/LZ48***

Fig 63. ***The protagonists; 2nd Lt Alfred de Bathe Brandon MC DSO MID (left) and Kapitänleutnant Joachim Breithaupt***

Fig 64. *The L15 after crashing into the sea from 'The War illustrated' April 1916*

The caption reads: *'THE DYING GASBAG, L15. –Vivid impression of Zeppelin L15 in her death-throes off the Thames estuary. Five of these cruisers of the skies raided Britain on the night of March 31st, two on April 1st, and six on April 2nd. The L15, one of the night-raiders of March 31st, was crippled either by gun fire or by bombs dropped by one of our airman at nine thousand feet. The colossal airship broke in the middle and fell from a great height into the sea. Patrol boats rescued seventeen of the crew, who quickly surrendered.'*

Unfortunately, there is no known personal account by Sir Charles Wakefield concerning the events surrounding the shooting down of the L15 or the award of the Wakefield Medals.

In March 1920, the Records Clerk at the Guildhall, Mr. A.H. Thomas, wrote to Sir Charles Wakefield regarding the possibility of the latter writing a history of his year in office. Sir Charles replied "I certainly hesitate very much to undertake to write the history of my year at the Mansion House as I am already tremendously overburdened with work."

As previously noted, if Sir Charles regarded the medals as a private matter, the story behind the award of these would almost certainly not have qualified for inclusion in an official history in any case.

CHARLES WAKEFIELD GOLD MEDAL POEM
By Simpleton

The R.F.C. Flyers were revered as Gods
The soldiers were ignored, poor sods
Captain Leefe Robinson was awarded the VC
The gunners were not offered a cup of tea!

Their Zeppelin fell into the North Sea surf
Londoners then called them, salt of the earth!
The Mayor of London had offered a cash prize
Angered by the Government, he had a surprise

He created a work of art, a wonder to behold
The Lord Wakefield Medal, 1oz of 9ct gold
353 medals were awarded to the gunners
Each with their name inscribed; not numbers.

OTHER WAKEFIELD MEDALS AND AWARDS

Sir Charles Wakefield supported many adventures in early aviation and sport. If you intend to undertake any research do be aware that there are other awards given in sporting events that were also named as The Wakefield Medal.

The earliest reference to a Wakefield award appears to be in 1911 when Charles Wakefield organized a competition for aero-models in the grounds of Crystal Palace, London. Wakefield had a gold cup made for the competition. The Wakefield Gold Cup contest of 1911 was won by a Mr Twining whose model was a canard type based on the theories of The Wright Brothers and an eccentric Brazilian called Alberto Santos Dumont.

Santos Dumont was a coffee plantation owner that lived in France. He built his own airships and flew them around the streets of Paris. Once he crashed his airship into a high building, and was left perched on a window ledge, unable to enter through the window as it had steel bars across it. He was rescued by firemen.

He built a total of 15 airships and on the 19th October 1901 won a monetary award of 100,000 francs flying his Santos Dumont no. 6. It was a set course of 7.5 miles which included rounding the Eiffel Tower. It only took him 29.5 minutes to complete the course.

On the 31st July 1903 Santos Dumont met with officers of the Ministere de la Guerre (Ministry of War) and he spoke about the advantages of airships in warfare. He advised that any submarine would be beautifully visible to an airship, while, from a warship's deck, it could not be seen. It would be the master of the situation for while the submarine cannot attack the airship the latter, having twice the speed, can find the submarine, follow its movements, and relay its position to the hunting warships. Dumont also proposed dropping arrows from airships filled with dynamite to destroy the submarines. This was the forerunner of the depth charge.

Fig 65. *The Wakefield RAF Boxing Trophy Medal in 9k gold*

The Wakefield Boxing Trophy was proposed by Sir

Charles Wakefield in November 1918 and is still contested by the RAF Boxing Association today. The original medals were manufactured by Vaughton of Birmingham. The medal illustrated was awarded to the Heavyweight Champion of 1937, Leading Aircraftman A. Tubbs.

During his year in office, as Lord Mayor, Sir Charles Wakefield also supported the Home Counties Cadet Battalions Football Association with the award of medals. The medals were struck in silver with an image of Sir Charles Wakefield in military uniform, on the obverse, and three soldiers with rifles on the reverse.

Fig 66. ***The Home Counties Cadet Battalions Football Association Medal***

This was awarded by Sir Charles Wakefield in his capacity as Lord Mayor of London

The medal below was instigated to commemorate the visit by Sir Charles Wakefield in the capacity of acting Lord Mayor, and a deputation from the Corporation of London, to Prague in 1920 to promote friendly trading relationships between the two cities.

The visit was a success and Sir Charles was subsequently awarded the Order of the White Lion of Czecho-Slovakia. The medal illustrated below was awarded to M H Crees for an essay on the subject of improvement to the economic situation in Czecho-Slovakia in 1922.

Fig 67. ***The Sir Charles Wakefield Prague Commemorative medal. Obverse***

Fig 68. ***The Sir Charles Wakefield Prague Commemorative medal. Reverse***

ZEPPELIN RELATED MEDALS & BADGES

The medal below, in hallmarked silver, was made by William James Dingley of Birmingham in 1920. It was presented by HOMCO (The Hull Oil Manufacturing Company of Stoneferry) to L Goodinson for 'services rendered' on 5th April 1916 during what is depicted on the medal as anti-aircraft defence.

It is not clear how many of these medals were struck or the circumstances surrounding their award.

Fig 69. ***HOMCO silver medal, 1.25 inches in diameter, presented to L Goodinson in 1920***

Fig 70. ***William James Dingley of Birmingham hallmark on the HOMCO silver medal***

It is not clear if L Goodison was an employee of HOMCO or one of a number of military personnel who received the same award.

It wasn't just the military who received awards in relation to air raids. A number of civilians, including nurses, air-raid wardens and the women operators at the London Telephone Service, who refused to leave their posts during the air raids to keep lines of communication open, were also recognised for their courage and dedication during the Zeppelin attacks.

The 9ct gold medal below was awarded to Miss Betty Randall a nurse with 218 (Lewisham) London Voluntary Aid Division for remaining at her post in Lewisham Hospital during a Zeppelin raid.

It was presented by the Mayoress of Lewisham.

Fig 71. VAD medal awarded to Miss Betty Randall in 1919 for air raid services during the Zeppelin attacks on London

The medal has a Vaughton's of Birmingham hallmark for 1919. As with the Homco medal illustrated above it was awarded several years after the action it related to.

Fig 72. ***Details of the Vaughton's of Birmingham 9ct gold hallmark on the VAD medal***

The medal below was presented to T. W. Homer, an air-raid warden, by the Metropolitan Borough of Wandsworth for services rendered during air raids 1915-1918.

Fig 73. ***Medal Awarded to T. W. Homer for services rendered during air raids 1915 - 1918***

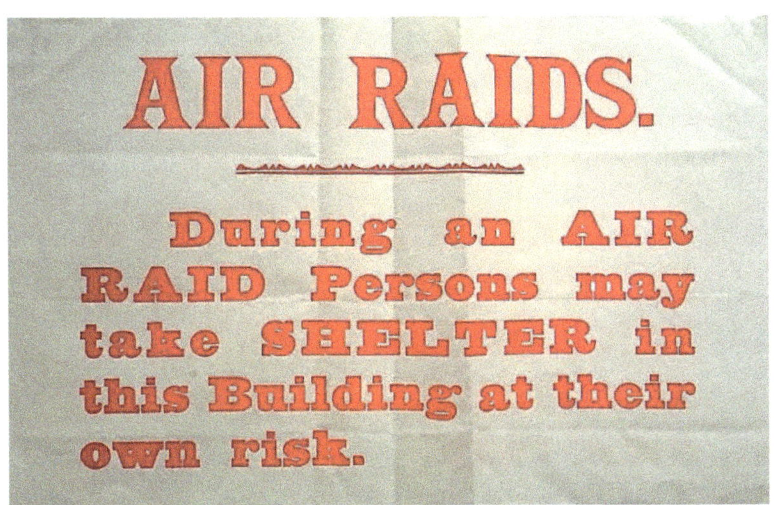

Fig 74. ***Air Raid warning poster 1916 – 1918***

Fig 75. ***London Telephone Service badge of distinction awarded by the Postmaster General***

This badge was awarded to female telephone operators of the London Telephone Service who remained at their posts to keep military lines of communication open during the Zeppelin raids

PART 3 - THE STORY OF THE LZ85 COMPASS

It was the chance discovery of this compass in a junk shop, in the 1960s, which first aroused my interest in Zeppelins and lighter-than-air flight.

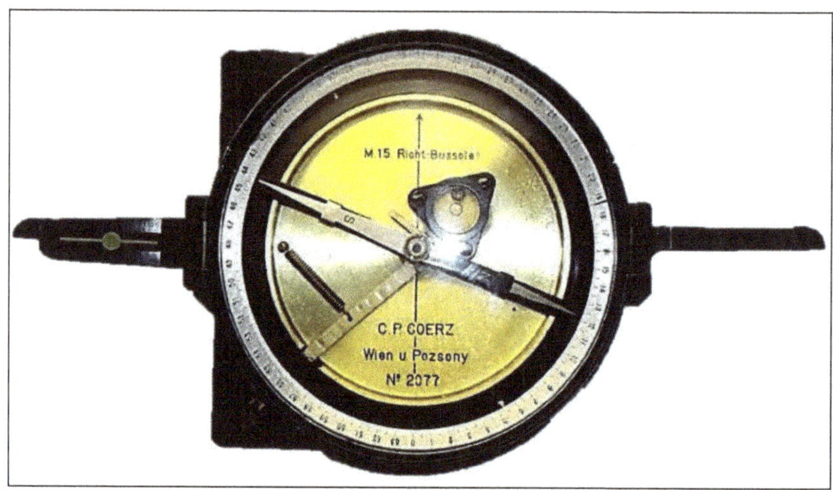

Fig 76. ***The Zeppelin compass no. 2077***

The Compass was manufactured by C. P. GOERZ on 1st January 1915 and was taken from the **LZ85/LZ55** at Salonika Greece.

LZ85 is the Zeppelin's military number and LZ55 is the maker's construction number.

The German production numbers of the airships were meant to be confusing as they did not want the British to know how many were produced.

There were two main factories for the manufacture of Airships in Germany; Luftshiffbau Zeppelin at Friedrichshafen and Schutte-Lanz at Bruhl. It is necessary to tell you something about the Ottoman Empire as the **LZ85/LZ55** Zeppelin compass, illustrated below, was taken from the crew after their airship was shot down at Salonika.

The port town now known as Thessaloniki, which is the capital of Greek Macedonia, is often referred to internationally as Salonica or Salonika. This article concerns the period of the First World War 1914-1918 when the British press used both spellings.

The city was founded in 315 BC by King Cassander who named it Thessalonika after his wife Thessalonike. In 168 BC it became part of the Roman Republic and was called Thessalonica. Thessaloniki was called Selanik in Turkish. In 1912 during the Balkan war the Ottoman garrison surrendered Salonika to the Greek army.

I shall use the spelling Salonika as this was used when the Allied Expeditionary Forces used Salonika as a base for an offensive against Bulgaria which was pro-German.

The **LZ85/LZ55** Zeppelin was a P Class. (An enlarged M Class) It had a volume of 1,126,389 cu ft (31,895.8m3). This type was the first airship produced in quantity after the outbreak of war. Twenty-two were built and twelve lengthened.

Zeppelins were once considered more useful and effective than aeroplanes. They were also very effective at spotting submarines. The first Zeppelin raids on England were on the 19th and 20th January 1915. Two Zeppelins **L3/LZ24** and **L4/LZ27** dropped twenty-four high explosive bombs and a number of incendiary bombs on Great Yarmouth, and Kings Lynn. Four people were killed and sixteen injured.

The finding of a compass in a junk shop over fifty years ago led to a long search for the origin and background to this incredible piece of engineering, its history and purpose, then to its journey through the First World War and how it came to be in my hands in England.

Anti-aircraft fire was often less than effective against the Zeppelins. It was not until the night of 2nd September 1916 that a Shutte-Lanz type of airship the **SL11** was shot down by a B.E.2c fighter aircraft flown by William Leefe Robinson using the new Brock and Pomeroy incendiary ammunition. He received the Victoria Cross.

I became totally fascinated with lighter than air flight, so much so that I became a hot air balloon pilot and flew across London from The Old Kent Road and by chance landed in Potters Bar at the end of Tempest Road where the Zeppelin **LZ72/L31** crashed on the 2nd October 1916 after being shot down by 2nd Lieutenant Wulstan Tempest of the RFC.

Fig 77. ***The crash site of the LZ72/L31 shot down at Potters Bar on 2nd October 1916***

The **LZ72/L31** crashed into a large oak tree which subsequently became known as the 'Zeppelin Oak'. Huge numbers of sightseers and souvenir hunters travelled to the site from London and the wreckage had to be protected by armed soldiers. The Captain and his entire crew lost their lives. 2nd Lieutenant Wulstan Tempest travelled to the site after landing and paid one shilling to enter the site anonymously. One can only wonder what his thoughts were as he viewed the wreckage for which he was responsible.

Following the destruction of the **LZ72/L31** airship the German Military command demanded Zeppelins to be capable of flying to altitudes of 25,000ft (7,600m). The Royal Flying Corps B.E.2c fighter aircraft was only capable of reaching a height of 10,560ft. The new Zeppelins were called 'Height-climbers'.

The **LZ85/LZ55** was originally launched in 1915 but then extensively enlarged to make it a height-climber in order to climb above enemy anti-aircraft fire. This was the reason it had a lightweight compass made for it. They also dispensed with defensive guns and parachutes. That enabled them to carry 8 x 66 lb Bombs, 16 x 200 lb and 60 incendiary bombs. A coating of black paint on the underside made them almost invisible at night.

In November 1917, Zeppelin 104 (its Imperial Navy Number was LZ59) based in Yamboz in Bulgaria was sent to supply German troops engaged in Paul von Lettow-Vorbecks East African Campaign in German East Africa. This is now Tanzania. The British said they had sent a false radio report that the Germans had suffered a defeat by the British troops and therefore the Zeppelin started its journey back to Bulgaria. It had travelled 4,200 miles (6,800km) in 95 hours. It could have stayed airborne another 64 hrs. It was nicknamed 'Das Africa Shiff'. This was an example of the technical ability of these wonderfully crafted airships. It was the wind and weather that were mostly responsible for their downfall.

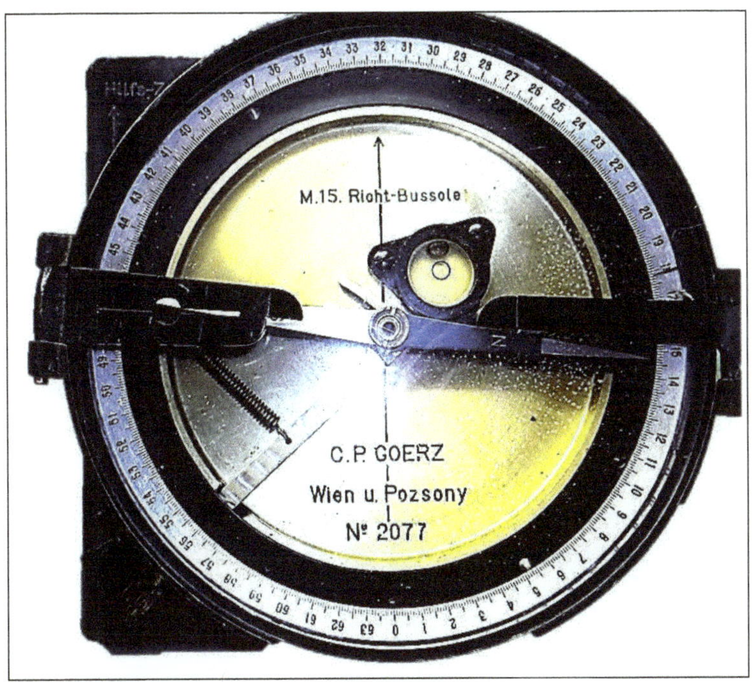

Fig 78. ***Close up of Zeppelin compass no. 2077***

I found the lightweight compass of the P class Zeppelin **LZ85/LZ55** when searching for altimeters to use for skydiving. It was in the 1960s that I wandered into a junk-shop in Badshot Lea, near Farnham, Surrey. This village is on the outskirts of the Military town of Aldershot. I was hoping to find military altimeters but I saw a compass. I knew that it was not a ship's compass and I was puzzled by the fact that it would not fit into an aircraft's instrument panel. I could see it was made in Germany and purchased it on an impulse for it had obviously been manufactured with great care and precision.

When I got home it occurred to me that it might have been used on a modern airship as it was not a heavy ship's compass. I had seen photographs of the Graf Zeppelin's compass that was huge. This one weighed 400 grams and measured 6in (150mm) across. It was much later that I looked at the inside of the lid that protects the glass and found a tiny but precise map of the Northern part of The Ottoman Empire. It was only then that I realized the compass was quite old and that it probably came from a military Zeppelin. Normally an item made for war would tend to be functional, ugly, but a Zeppelin was something that I felt was beautiful when it floated through the skies. All that saw it wanted to be flying in it. I must add that if it was bombing you, your feelings would be quite different.

Seeing the map within the compass made me inquire about the Balkans war. The Austrian Hungary offensive was met with strong Serbian resistance. Serbia's fate was sealed by the middle of 1915 by two factors; Germany's interest in maintaining its relationship with Turkey and Bulgaria's entry into the war.

The LZ85 had a works or manufacturing number of LZ55 and it was launched in 1915 but was then enlarged to a volume of 1,264,100cu ft 35,795m^3) with a length of 585ft (178m) and diameter of 61.3ft

(18.69m). It was powered by four Maybach 210hp (160kW) engines with a maximum airspeed of 60.1mph (96.7km/h). This was to give it a high operational ceiling to avoid the RFC fighters and the anti-aircraft guns.

The numbering can be quite confusing but I believe that this was done deliberately to confuse British Intelligence about the number of Airships built. There were two Zeppelins listed as LZ85 the reason being there was the builder's number and the Army registration number. The LZ85 I am writing about was a P Class launched in 1915.

THE MAP INSIDE THE COMPASS LID

I researched the cities and towns engraved in the metal map in the lid. These comprised, starting on the eastern side the Adriatic Sea, Tirane (Tirana) in Albania, Sarajevo and Beograd (Belgrade) Yugoslavia, Triest, Zara, City and seaport in North Eastern Italy on the border with Slovenia. Innsbruck, capital City of The Tyrol in Western Austria, Klagenfurt Airport founded as a Military Airport in 1914. Praha, (Prague) in the Czech Republic, it also shows the Elbe. Krakau (Krakow) Poland and also shown is Warshau (Warsaw).

Warsaw was bombed by the Shutte-lanz **SL2** Airship in 1914. Warsaw was the Polish capital during Russian rule and was occupied by Germany from 4th August 1915 until 1918.

Lemberg in the Ukraine is now called Lviv. In September 1914 Lemberg was captured by the Russians. Moving down the Black Sea coast there is Bukarest (Budapest) Romania, and Contana which was occupied by German and Turkish troops on 22nd October 1916. In August 1914 when the First World War broke out Romania tried to remain neutral but joined the Allies on 27th August 1916. At the base or south of the map there is shown Thessaloniki (Salonika) on the Aegean Sea. The date on the map is marked 'Wien 1.Janner.1915'. That fits with the date of the launch of the LZ85 which was built with the construction number LZ55.

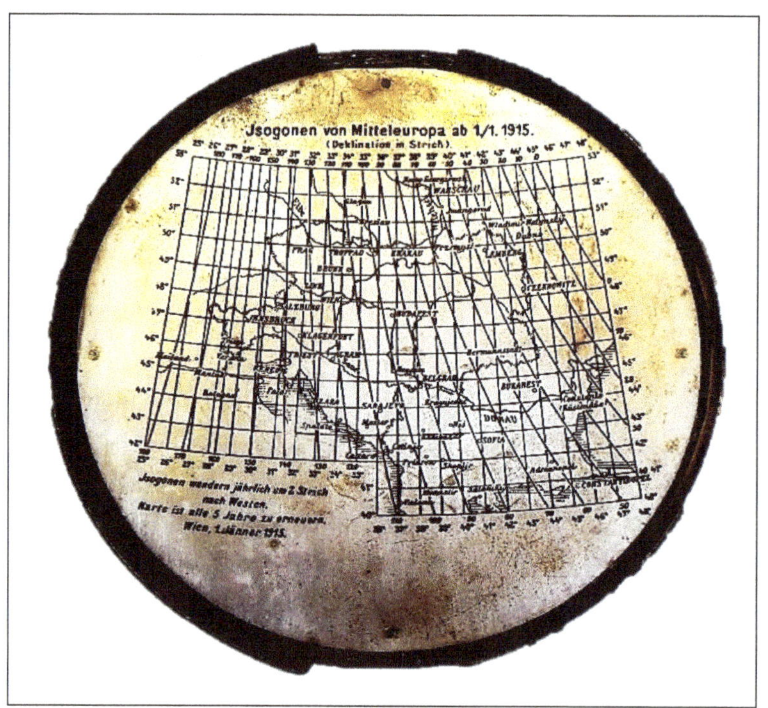

Fig 79. ***Close up of the LZ85/LZ55 compass lid***

The date inscribed in the compass lid is the 1st January 1915. The **LZ85/LZ55** was launched later in 1915. On the previous page I have illustrated the detachable lid of the compass with the map inscribed inside. The image below shows more of the detail. It covers Western Europe and the area that the Zeppelin was going to operate in. As with most Zeppelins in the First World War it did not survive very long, but the Zeppelins did instil fear in the populations that they bombed.

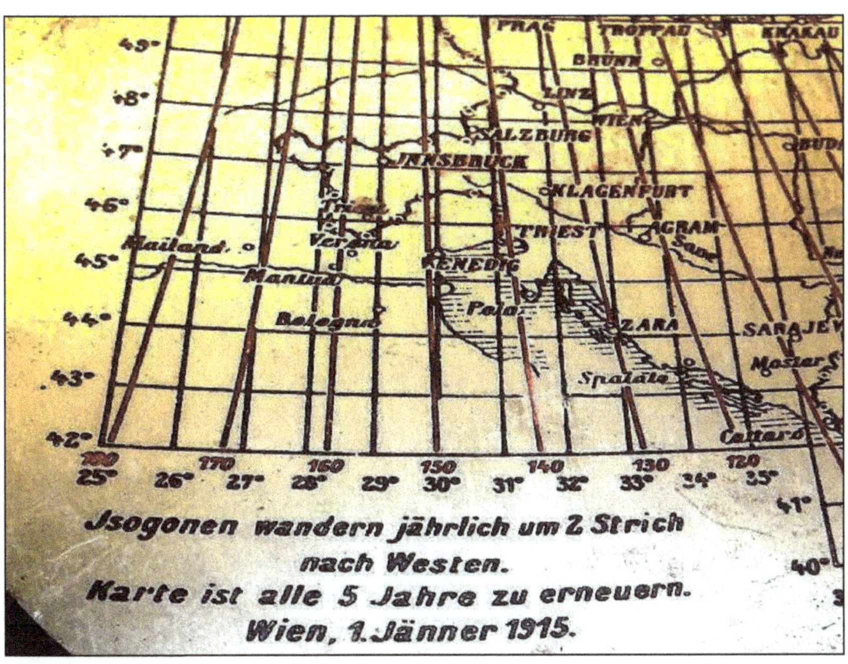

Fig 80. ***The LZ85/LZ55 compass lid showing the fine detail of the map***

Salonika was part of the Ottoman Empire. On the 8th November 1912 the Greek Army accepted the surrender of The Ottoman Garrison at Thessaloniki

(Salonika). In 1915 a large Expeditionary force established a base at Salonika for operations against pro-German Bulgaria. This proves that this compass was intended to be used on operations in this region.

The compass was manufactured by C.P.Goerz of Wien (Vienna) Wien u Pozsony. It is numbered 2077 on the lid and on the face M.15. Right-Bussole. In the top left hand corner is Hilfe-Ziel and the compass was made to slot and clip on to an instrument panel.

On the base is crudely stamped - OK 10.5.16. And a mark that appears to be the British Royal Marines emblem. This date on the base of 10.5.16 is five days after the **LZ85/LZ55** was shot down and after the crew were captured by the British Royal Marines which were from the TB18 Motor torpedo boat. They would stamp their mark on everything that came into their possession.

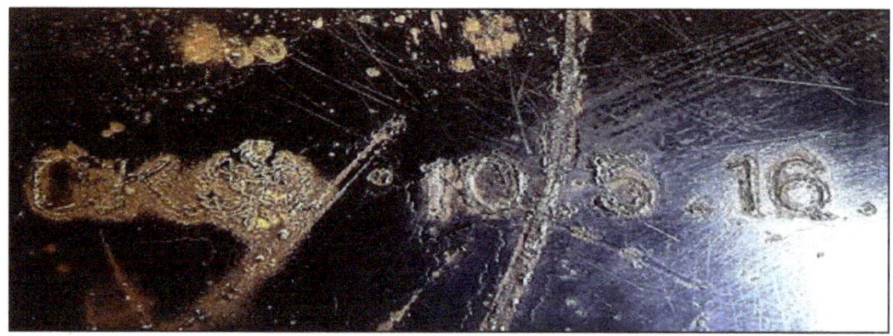

Fig 81. ***Reverse of the compass showing the Royal Marines date mark***

THE SALONIKA EXPEDITIONARY FORCE

British and Commonwealth troops were sent to Salonika in 1915 to help the Serbians, they arrived in Salonika on 3rd October 1915 but it was too late and they ended up fighting the Bulgarian Army.

It was called an expeditionary force and they ended up making a withdrawal, but it was a disaster with 44,150 allied soldiers killed and another 97,397 wounded.

The total Allied casualties, according to the official figures, were 141,547. Only one officer and eighteen men survived from the 7th South Wales Borderers which would have consisted of about 1,000 men.

THE GALLIPOLI CAMPAIGN

February - November 1915. This was the Allied campaign to gain control of the Dardanelles. It was an attempt by sea and land to capture Constantinople (Istanbul) and to remove Turkey from the war. The bombardment of Turkish defences started in February 1915.

There was a loss of five Allied battleships to Turkish mines and gunfire so by November 1915 the operation was abandoned. The military leaders were now paying their attention to the war on the Western Front. One of the British Battleships involved in the Dardanelles was *HMS Agamemnon.*

Fig 82. ***A postcard showing HMS Agamemnon***

It was on the 28th December 1916 that the crew of the British Battleship *HMS Agamemnon* were advised that they were to be withdrawn from the campaign. This campaign is recorded as being of the period between April 1915 to January 1916 and left 24,000 British and Commonwealth troops dead and out of twelve British and French submarines, which entered the Sea of Marmara, six were sunk. The British submarines were the E7, E15, and the E20. There were also four British battleships and one French battleship sunk.

It was on the 6th May 1916 that this British Battleship *H.M.S. Agamemnon*, flagship of the Mediterranean fleet, was anchored in the harbour at Salonika. This Battleship, commissioned in 1908, was one of two Lord Nelson class ships and the last pre-Dreadnought Class and weighed 16,500 tons.

She was armed with four 12 inch guns, ten 9.2 inch guns, fifteen 12 pounder guns, sixteen small quick firing guns, and five torpedo tubes.

Zeppelin Captain Ernst Sherzer had already taken part in three raids against Russia, at Dunnaberg, Riga and Minsk in October 1915. After taking command of the **LZ85/LZ55** he had already flown from Temesvar in Romania on the 27th January 1916 to successfully bomb Salonika.

He then struck again on the 17th March 1916. It was during his third raid on Salonika that his luck finally ran out. Captain Sherzer made a serious mistake by flying low over Salonika where two men and one gun on *HMS Agamemnon* brought the **LZ85/LZ55** down into the Vardar marshes at Salonika in Greece on the 5th May 1916.

The ship was not on action stations when the **LZ85/LZ55** flew over the harbour but Lt Cruickshank and Leading Seaman Coleman loaded and fired at the Zeppelin with a 12 pounder gun. This was mounted on a high carriage on the forward bridge of HMS Agamemnon. The shell tore through the gas bags of the **LZ85/LZ55** and caused it to lose buoyancy and it came down in the remote Vardar marshes.

Fig 83. ***Lt Cruickshank and Leading Seaman Coleman HMS Agamemnon***

This photograph shows the 12 pounder gun on the *HMS Agamemnon* used to shoot down the **LZ85/LZ55**. (Courtesy of *The Times History and Encyclopaedia of the War*)

Lt Cruickshank was killed some years later by an elephant whilst on an expedition in Tanganyika.

MOTOR TORPEDO BOAT TB18

It was recorded that the British Motor Torpedo boat TB18 also managed to score a hit. This could only have been as the Zeppelin descended into the marshes. This was the MTB crew and marines that chased into the marshes looking for the German airship crew. (TB18 referred to the single 18 inch diameter torpedo it carried) This would not be the relatively small Motor-torpedo boats used in WW2 but much larger craft with the torpedo at the stern so they had to turn around to aim and fire it.

The Zeppelin crew set fire to the airship after they landed and then attempted to escape through the marshes. This was to prove extremely difficult, for the average depth of water was waist high and reeds towered above their heads. It is obvious that they would have taken any compasses with them on their journey.

According to an account written by an eye witness, directly the Zeppelin came down a British torpedo boat patrolling in the area, landed a party to arrest the crew and remove anything of importance from the wreck. It appears that the French Cavalry then re-arrested the crew and they were taken to the French prisoner of war camp in Salonika. They were then handed back over to the British who interrogated the crew from 15th December 1916 until 20th December 1916.

Fig 84. ***French Army and British Naval Officers inspecting the burnt remains of the LZ85/LZ55 Zeppelin in the Vardar Marshes***

Note that they are standing in water. Apparently even British nurses trudged through the marsh to get pieces of the wreckage and it was not an easy task as one male officer drowned doing so even though he was on a horse.

The remains of the **LZ85/LZ55** were dismantled in the Vardar marshes, transported to Salonika harbour, and reassembled on the harbour wall to study its construction. It was later transported to Barrow-in-Furness, in England, by the Observation Balloon Ship HMS Canning. The remains were then studied to assist in the design of British airships.

Fig 85. ***Postcard of the LZ85/LZ55 wreckage on the harbour wall at Salonika in Greece***

When I first picked up this postcard I thought it was part of a fairground attraction.

Fig 86. ***A postcard showing members of the captured crew of the LZ85/LZ55***

The crew was handed over to the French authorities for questioning before being returned to the British Military Authorities. Eventually the crew was transported by sea to France. There were thirteen members in total; Hauptman Ernst Scherzer, Oberleutnant Werner Nippe, Leutnant Thelen, Lt. Bernhard Noak, Anton Katzemaier, Herman Kuck, Wilhelm Mertens, Peter Bervenich, Wilhelm Lautenback, Heinrich Kaiser, Adolf Schmidt, Adolf Ehrlich and Fritz Streyreiff.

Fig 87. ***A postcard from the Balkans***

The above postcard, posted from the Army Post Office S.X.12 SALONICA on the 11th December 1917 and passed by Censor No. 420 made it look like it was a dream holiday but it was a nightmare.

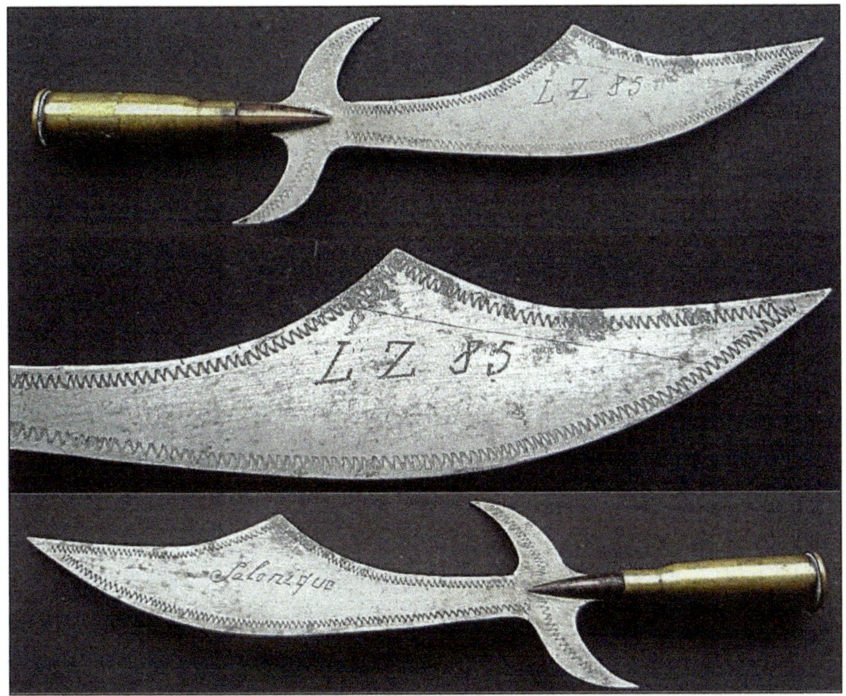

Fig 88. ***Trench art letter opener made from a piece of the LZ85 Zeppelin***

By pure chance I also acquired a letter opener made by a soldier from a WW1 rifle bullet and a piece of the **LZ85/LZ55** Zeppelin. It has 'LZ85' engraved on one side of the blade and 'Salonique' on the other.

CONCLUSION

I hope that you have found these stories an interesting journey through not only the politics of war, machines of war and the combatants' experiences, but also the suffering of the unfortunate victims.

BIBLIOGRAPHY

Gott Strafe England: The German air assault against Great Britain 1914-1918 Volume 1. By Parker, Nigel J. Helion and Company 2015. ISBN-13: 978-1909982710

LONDON 1914-17: The Zeppelin Menace (Campaign 193). By Castle, Ian. Osprey 2008. ISBN-13: 978-1846032455

The Zeppelin in Combat. By Robinson, Douglas. G. T. Foulis & Co. 1971. ISBN-13: 978-0854291304

Zeppelin Nights. London in the First World War. By White, Jerry. Bodley Head 2014. ISBN-13: 978-1847921659

Air Raids on South West Essex in the Great War: Looking for Zeppelins at Leyton. By Simpson, Alan David. Pen & Sword Aviation 2015. ISBN-13: 978-1473834125

Zeppelins against London. By Poolman, Kenneth. John Day 1961. ASIN: B0007DZSBG

The First Blitz: Bombing London in the First World War. By Castle, Ian. Osprey 2015. ISBN-13: 978-1472815293

The Zeppelins: The Development of the Airship, with the Story of the Zeppelin Air Raids in the

World War. By Lehmann, Ernst A. and Mingos Howard. G.P. Putnam 1927. ASIN: B001OXY4A4

Zeppelin vs British Home Defence 1915–18 (Duel). By Guttman, Jon. Osprey 2018. ISBN-13: 978-1472820334

Hornchurch's Air Heroes of the First World War: A Pictorial History of Royal Flying Corps, Sutton's Farm 1915-1919. By Smith, Richard C. Mitor Publications 2014. ISBN-13: 978-0955718045

The Defence of London 1915-1918. By Rawlinson A. Melrose 1924. ASIN: B001NK4I7M

Jane's Pocket Book of Airship Development By Lord Ventry and Eugène M. Koleśnik. Macdonald and Jane's 1976. ISBN 0356 04656 7

The Commercial Motor
November 16th 1916 Edition

Royal United Services Institute Journal
Volume 95, Issue 759, August 1950. Article *The Destruction of Zeppelin L.15 – An early A.A. Success* by Brigadier H.B. Latham.

The Royal Arsenal Railways: The Rise and Fall of a Military Railway Network. By Mark Smithers. Pen and Sword Books Ltd. 2016. ISBN-13: 978-1473844001

APPENDIX 1 – ALPHABETICAL LIST OF RECIPIENTS OF THE SIR CHARLES WAKEFIELD GOLD MEDAL 1916

Surname	Forenames	Rank	Number	Corps or Regiment
AFFLEY	T	Corporal		2 Company Glamorgan RGA (TF) Southern Outfall and Plumstead Common
ALLAN	F	Sapper		Tyne Electrical Engineers RA (TF) (Searchlights) Darenth
ALLAWAY	Sidney Alfred			Not known
ALLEN	J	Gunner		5 Company Cornwall RGA (TF) Erith and Dartford
ALLEN	S	Gunner		5 Company Cornwall RGA (TF) Erith and Dartford
ANDERSON		Gunner		2 Company Glamorgan RGA (TF) Southern

				Outfall and Plumstead Common
ARMSTRONG	S	L/Corporal		Tyne Electrical Engineers RA (TF) (Searchlights) Darenth
ARTHUR	A	Sergeant		Regulars and "K" Army RA Abbey Wood (Lessness Abbey)
ATWOOD		Gunner		3 Company Essex and Suffolk RGA (TF) Purfleet
AVERY	A	Sergeant		2 Company Glamorgan RGA (TF) Southern Outfall and Plumstead Common
BALL	F	Trumpeter		2 Company Glamorgan RGA (TF) Southern Outfall and Plumstead Common
BARNES		Gunner		2 Company Glamorgan RGA (TF) Southern Outfall and

				Plumstead Common
BARNETT	R N	Lieutenant		2 Company Glamorgan RGA (TF) Southern Outfall and Plumstead Common
BARRY	H	Gunner		2 Company Glamorgan RGA (TF) Southern Outfall and Plumstead Common
BEALE		Corporal		3 Company Essex and Suffolk RGA (TF) Purfleet
BERRYMAN	J	Gunner		5 Company Cornwall RGA (TF) Erith and Dartford
BIRD	H	Bombardier		2 Company Glamorgan RGA (TF) Southern Outfall and Plumstead Common
BERRILL	W	Gunner		2nd Coy Glamorgan RGA (TF) Southern Outfall and

				Plumstead Common
BICHENO	Charles	Gunner		Not known
BIRCH	Harry	Gunner		Not known
BIRRELL		Gunner		3 Company Essex and Suffolk RGA (TF) Purfleet
BIRRELL		Gunner		3 Company Essex and Suffolk RGA (TF) Purfleet
BISHOP		Gunner		5 Company Cornwall RGA (TF) Erith and Dartford
BOLT	P	Corporal		Tyne Electrical Engineers RA (TF) (Searchlights) Darenth
BOSHIER	A	Gunner		2 Company Glamorgan RGA (TF) Southern Outfall and Plumstead Common
BOWEN	J	Gunner		2 Company Glamorgan RGA (TF) Southern Outfall and Plumstead

				Common
BREWER	A	Gunner		2 Company Glamorgan RGA (TF) Southern Outfall and Plumstead Common
BROCK	E	Sergeant		2 Company Glamorgan RGA (TF) Southern Outfall and Plumstead Common
BROOMFIELD	C	Gunner		2 Company Glamorgan RGA (TF) Southern Outfall and Plumstead Common
BROWN	C	Corporal		Not known
BUTLER		Gunner		Not known
CALLAGHAN	E	Gunner		2 Company Glamorgan RGA (TF) Southern Outfall and Plumstead Common
CALLAGHAN	R	Bombardier		Not known
CARTHEW	T	Gunner		5 Company Cornwall RGA (TF) Erith and

				Dartford
CAUSER	D S	2nd Lieutenant		5 Company Cornwall RGA (TF) Erith and Dartford
CHIDGEY		Gunner		2 Company Glamorgan RGA (TF) Southern Outfall and Plumstead Common
CLARKE		Gunner		3 Company Essex and Suffolk RGA (TF) Purfleet
COCKING		Gunner		5 Company Cornwall RGA (TF) Erith and Dartford
COGGER	S	Gunner		3 Company Essex and Suffolk RGA (TF) Purfleet
COGGINS	G	Gunner		2 Company Glamorgan RGA (TF) Southern Outfall and Plumstead Common
COLMAN	Oliver John	Driver	S4/1293 49	Army Service Corps
COOPER	George H	Sergeant		Not known

COPE	W	Gunner		2 Company Glamorgan RGA (TF) Southern Outfall and Plumstead Common
COTHEY	J	Gunner		5 Company Cornwall RGA (TF) Erith and Dartford
COUCH	R	Gunner		5 Company Cornwall RGA (TF) Erith and Dartford
COX	J	Gunner		2 Company Glamorgan RGA (TF) Southern Outfall and Plumstead Common
COX		Gunner		Not known
CREEMER	F	Corporal		2 Company Glamorgan RGA (TF) Southern Outfall and Plumstead Common
CRIMMINGS	D	Gunner		2 Company Glamorgan RGA (TF) Southern Outfall and

				Plumstead Common
CURTIS	E	Gunner		2 Company Glamorgan RGA (TF) Southern Outfall and Plumstead Common
CURTIS	W J	Gunner		2 Company Glamorgan RGA (TF) Southern Outfall and Plumstead Common
CUSHWAY	A J	Sapper		6 Company London Electrical Engineers RE (TF) (Searchlights)
DARGAN	F	Gunner		RGA
DAVE		Bombardier		5 Company Cornwall RGA (TF) Erith and Dartford
DAWKINS		Bombardier		3 Company Essex and Suffolk RGA (TF) Purfleet
DAWKINS		Gunner		3 Company Essex and Suffolk RGA (TF) Purfleet
DE BATH	Alfred	2nd		Royal Flying

BRANDON		Lieutenant		Corps
DELVE	C	Gunner		5 Company Cornwall RGA (TF) Erith and Dartford
DERBYSHIRE		Gunner		3 Company Essex and Suffolk RGA (TF) Purfleet
DONAGHUE		Gunner		2 Company Glamorgan RGA (TF) Southern Outfall and Plumstead Common
DONALDSON	J	Sergeant		Tyne Electrical Engineers RA (TF) (Searchlights) Darenth
DORKINS	G M	Corporal		3 Company Essex and Suffolk RGA (TF) Purfleet
DORKINS	R L	Gunner		3 Company Essex and Suffolk RGA (TF) Purfleet
DOWNER		Corporal		3 Company Essex and Suffolk RGA (TF) Purfleet
DREW	Arthur Edward			Not known

DUDGEON		2nd Lieutenant		5 Company Cornwall RGA (TF) Erith and Dartford
DUNSCOMBE	A	Gunner		2 Company Glamorgan RGA (TF) Southern Outfall and Plumstead Common
DUNSTON		Gunner		5 Company Cornwall RGA (TF) Erith and Dartford
EARL	H M	Sapper		Royal Engineers TRE London
EDDY	Edward John	Gunner		5 Company Cornwall RGA (TF) Erith and Dartford
EDWARDS		Gunner		3 Company Essex and Suffolk RGA (TF) Purfleet
ELLIOTT	E	Corporal		2 Company Glamorgan RGA (TF) Southern Outfall and Plumstead Common
ELLIOTT	R	Sapper		Tyne

				Electrical Engineers RA (TF) (Searchlights) Darenth
ESSEX	J	Gunner		2 Company Glamorgan RGA (TF) Southern Outfall and Plumstead Common
EVANS	D	Gunner		2 Company Glamorgan RGA (TF) Southern Outfall and Plumstead Common
EVANS	F	Gunner		2 Company Glamorgan RGA (TF) Southern Outfall and Plumstead Common
EVANS	H W	Corporal		2 Company Glamorgan RGA (TF) Southern Outfall and Plumstead Common
EVANS	R	Gunner		Not known
EVANS		Gunner		3 Company Essex and Suffolk RGA

				(TF) Purfleet
FISH		Gunner		3 Company Essex and Suffolk RGA (TF) Purfleet
FLACK		Gunner		3 Company Essex and Suffolk RGA (TF) Purfleet
FOX		Lieutenant		3 Company Essex and Suffolk RGA (TF) Purfleet
FREEMAN		Gunner		5 Company Cornwall RGA (TF) Erith and Dartford
FRENCH		Sergeant		3 Company Essex and Suffolk RGA (TF) Purfleet
FRY		Gunner		North Woolwich
GABB	I	Gunner		2 Company Glamorgan RGA (TF) Southern Outfall and Plumstead Common
GEACH	W	Gunner		5 Company Cornwall RGA (TF) Erith and Dartford

GILBERT	F	Gunner		5 Company Cornwall RGA (TF) Erith and Dartford
GLADWELL	Albert Charles	Gunner	707 118706	3 Company Essex and Suffolk RGA (TF) Purfleet
GLADWIN		Gunner		3 Company Essex and Suffolk RGA (TF) Purfleet
GODDARD		Gunner		3 Company Essex and Suffolk RGA (TF) Purfleet
GOODARD		Gunner		3 Company Essex and Suffolk RGA (TF) Purfleet
GOMER	P	Gunner		2 Company Glamorgan RGA (TF) Southern Outfall and Plumstead Common
GOUGH	T	Gunner		2 Company Glamorgan RGA (TF) Southern Outfall and Plumstead Common
GREEN		Gunner		3 Company Essex and

				Suffolk RGA (TF) Purfleet
GREENWAY	G	Lieutenant		2 Company Glamorgan RGA (TF) Southern Outfall and Plumstead Common
GRONOW	P	Gunner		2 Company Glamorgan RGA (TF) Southern Outfall and Plumstead Common
GRUMBRIDGE	G	CQMS		2 Company Glamorgan RGA (TF) Southern Outfall and Plumstead Common
GUEST	W A	Corporal		6 Company London Electrical Engineers RE (TF) (Searchlights)
GUIVER	V	Sergeant		3 Company Essex and Suffolk RGA (TF) Purfleet
GUNNING-CARR	A	Captain		2 Company Glamorgan RGA (TF) Southern

				Outfall and Plumstead Common
HAINES		Gunner		2 Company Glamorgan RGA (TF) Southern Outfall and Plumstead Common
HAMMANT	Walter R	Sapper	1589	Royal Engineers
HANCOCK	Clifford	Gunner	197	Royal Garrison Artillery
HANCOCK	G	Gunner		2 Company Glamorgan RGA (TF) Southern Outfall and Plumstead Common
HARPER		BSM		2 Company Glamorgan RGA (TF) Southern Outfall and Plumstead Common
HARRIS	Joseph	Captain		3 Company Essex and Suffolk RGA (TF) Purfleet
HARRIS	W	Gunner		5 Company Cornwall RGA (TF) Erith and

				Dartford
HARRIS		Gunner		5 Company Cornwall RGA (TF) Erith and Dartford
HARVEY		Gunner		2 Company Glamorgan RGA (TF) Southern Outfall and Plumstead Common
HASTINGS	L	Sapper		Tyne Electrical Engineers RA (TF) (Searchlights) Darenth
HEARING	Robert H	Gunner	59945	Not known
HESKETH		Gunner		Not known
HILL	F	Gunner		2 Company Glamorgan RGA (TF) Southern Outfall and Plumstead Common
HILL	T	Gunner		5 Company Cornwall RGA (TF) Erith and Dartford
HINKSMAN	W H	Gunner		2 Company Glamorgan RGA (TF)

				Southern Outfall and Plumstead Common
HODGE	S	Bombardier		5 Company Cornwall RGA (TF) Erith and Dartford
HODGINS	Arthur Wilfred Marrable	Lieutenant		Royal Garrison Artillery
HOGAN	Frank Thomas	Sapper		Royal Engineers
HOGAN	J	Sapper		Royal Engineers
HOLLAND		Gunner		3 Company Essex and Suffolk RGA (TF) Purfleet
HOLLOW		Gunner		Royal Garrison Artillery
HOLMES	W	Sergeant		2 Company Glamorgan RGA (TF) Southern Outfall and Plumstead Common
HOOPER	G	Gunner		2 Company Glamorgan RGA (TF) Southern Outfall and Plumstead

				Common
HOOPER		Gunner		3 Company Essex and Suffolk RGA (TF) Purfleet
HOPE	T	Gunner		2 Company Glamorgan RGA (TF) Southern Outfall and Plumstead Common
HORSLEY		Gunner		3 Company Essex and Suffolk RGA (TF) Purfleet
HOSEGOOD		Gunner		Not known
HOWARD	P H	Staff Sergeant		6 Company London Electrical Engineers RE (TF) (Searchlights)
HOWERD	L G	Lieutenant		3 Company Essex and Suffolk RGA (TF) Purfleet
HUNTER	E B	Captain		6 Company London Electrical Engineers RE (TF) (Searchlights)
INGRAM		Lieutenant		Regulars and "K" Army RA Abbey Wood (Lessness

				Abbey)
IRELAND	Alfred	Gunner		Royal Garrison Artillery
IRELAND		Gunner		Regulars and "K" Army RA Abbey Wood (Lessness Abbey)
JAMES	S	Bombardier		5 Company Cornwall RGA (TF) Erith and Dartford
JAMES		Gunner		5 Company Cornwall RGA (TF) Erith and Dartford
JOHN	L	Gunner		2 Company Glamorgan RGA (TF) Southern Outfall and Plumstead Common
JONES	E	Gunner		2 Company Glamorgan RGA (TF) Southern Outfall and Plumstead Common
JONES	W	Gunner		2 Company Glamorgan RGA (TF) Southern

				Outfall and Plumstead Common
JOSCELYNE	F	RQMS		3 Company Essex and Suffolk RGA (TF) Purfleet
JOSE	R	Gunner		5 Company Cornwall RGA (TF) Erith and Dartford
JULIEN	F	Gunner		Regulars and "K" Army RA Abbey Wood (Lessness Abbey)
KIDD		Gunner		3 Company Essex and Suffolk RGA (TF) Purfleet
KING	John J	Sapper		Tyne Electrical Engineers RA (TF) (Searchlights) Darenth
KING		Gunner		3 Company Essex and Suffolk RGA (TF) Purfleet
LAIRD		Lieutenant		3 Company Essex and Suffolk RGA (TF) Purfleet

LANGDON		Gunner		3 Company Essex and Suffolk RGA (TF) Purfleet
LAZELL		Gunner		3 Company Essex and Suffolk RGA (TF) Purfleet
LEWIS	C T B	Gunner		2 Company Glamorgan RGA (TF) Southern Outfall and Plumstead Common
LEWIS	E	Gunner		2 Company Glamorgan RGA (TF) Southern Outfall and Plumstead Common
LEWIS	W	Trumpeter		2 Company Glamorgan RGA (TF) Southern Outfall and Plumstead Common
LEWIS		Gunner		3 Company Essex and Suffolk RGA (TF) Purfleet
LEWIS		Gunner		Regulars and "K" Army RA Abbey Wood (Lessness

				Abbey)
LIVERMORE		Gunner		3 Company Essex and Suffolk RGA (TF) Purfleet
LUGG		Gunner		5 Company Cornwall RGA (TF) Erith and Dartford
MARCH	C	Gunner		2 Company Glamorgan RGA (TF) Southern Outfall and Plumstead Common
MARFELL	T	Gunner		2 Company Glamorgan RGA (TF) Southern Outfall and Plumstead Common
MARTIN		Gunner		5 Company Cornwall RGA (TF) Erith and Dartford
MAY	W	Gunner		2 Company Glamorgan RGA (TF) Southern Outfall and Plumstead Common
MCCANN		Sapper		Royal

				Engineers
MCDONALD		Gunner		2 Company Glamorgan RGA (TF) Southern Outfall and Plumstead Common
MCDONALD		Gunner		2 Company Glamorgan RGA (TF) Southern Outfall and Plumstead Common
MERRIFIELD		Gunner		Not known
MILDREN	W H	Gunner		5 Company Cornwall RGA (TF) Erith and Dartford
MOFFAT		Lieutenant		5 Company Cornwall RGA (TF) Erith and Dartford
MOORE		Gunner		3 Company Essex and Suffolk RGA (TF) Purfleet
MORGAN		Gunner		2 Company Glamorgan RGA (TF) Southern Outfall and Plumstead Common

MORGAN		Gunner		Not known
MUNRO	A	Gunner		2 Company Glamorgan RGA (TF) Southern Outfall and Plumstead Common
MURRAY		Gunner		Not known
NETHERCOTE	Walter Harold	Gunner		3 Company Essex and Suffolk RGA (TF) Purfleet
NEWTON		Lieutenant		3 Company Essex and Suffolk RGA (TF) Purfleet
NICHOLS	J	Gunner		2 Company Glamorgan RGA (TF) Southern Outfall and Plumstead Common
NOSEGOOD		Gunner		Regulars and "K" Army RA Abbey Wood (Lessness Abbey)
OAKLEY	W	Gunner		2 Company Glamorgan RGA (TF) Southern Outfall and Plumstead Common
O'KEEFE		Gunner		Not known

PAGE	G	Gunner		2 Company Glamorgan RGA (TF) Southern Outfall and Plumstead Common
PAGE	W	Gunner		2 Company Glamorgan RGA (TF) Southern Outfall and Plumstead Common
PANLIS	R	Gunner		5 Company Cornwall RGA (TF) Erith and Dartford
PANLIS	W	Gunner		5 Company Cornwall RGA (TF) Erith and Dartford
PARKER	J F	Sapper		Royal Engineers
PARKHOUSE	W	Gunner		2 Company Glamorgan RGA (TF) Southern Outfall and Plumstead Common
PAYNTER		Gunner		5 Company Cornwall RGA (TF) Erith and

				Dartford
PEACH	E	Gunner		2 Company Glamorgan RGA (TF) Southern Outfall and Plumstead Common
PEARCE	A H	Corporal		Royal Garrison Artillery
PEARCE	Alfred J	Gunner	20412	Royal Garrison Artillery
PEARCE	F D	Captain		Kent RGA (TF) Royal Arsenal Defences
PENFOLD	H J	Corporal		Royal Garrison Artillery
PHILLIPS	William	Bombardier		Not known
PHILLIPS		Gunner		3 Company Essex and Suffolk RGA (TF) Purfleet
POPE	T	Gunner		2 Company Glamorgan RGA (TF) Southern Outfall and Plumstead Common
PRING	W I	Lieutenant		2 Company Glamorgan RGA (TF)

				Southern Outfall and Plumstead Common
REYNOLDS	T	Gunner		3 Company Essex and Suffolk RGA (TF) Purfleet
RICHARDS		Sergeant		5 Company Cornwall RGA (TF) Erith and Dartford
RICHARDS	Richard James (Jim)	Gunner		2 Company Glamorgan RGA (TF) Southern Outfall and Plumstead Common
RIDD	J	Gunner		3 Company Essex and Suffolk RGA (TF) Purfleet
RILEY		Gunner		Regulars and "K" Army RA Abbey Wood (Lessness Abbey)
ROLLING	Stanley C	Gunner	321804	5 Company Cornwall RGA
ROSE	H J J	Driver		Army Service Corps
ROUSE	J H	Sapper		6 Company London Electrical

				Engineers RE (TF) (Searchlights)
RUTTER	H T	Sergeant		5 Company Cornwall RGA (TF) Erith and Dartford
SAMPSON	E	Gunner		5 Company Cornwall RGA (TF) Erith and Dartford
SARGENT	A	Bombardier		Regulars and "K" Army RA Abbey Wood (Lessness Abbey)
SAYERS		Gunner		3 Company Essex and Suffolk RGA (TF) Purfleet
SCRASE	F W	Private		Not known
SEMMENS	W	Gunner		5 Company Cornwall RGA (TF) Erith and Dartford
SHAWCROSS	Herbert	Bombardier	58592	Royal Garrison Artillery
SHELLEY		Gunner		3 Company Essex and Suffolk RGA (TF) Purfleet

SIRLEY	B	Gunner		Regulars and "K" Army RA Abbey Wood (Lessness Abbey)
SMITH	F H	Gunner		5 Company Cornwall RGA (TF) Erith and Dartford
SMITH		Lieutenant		Not known
SOWDEN		Gunner		5 Company Cornwall RGA (TF) Erith and Dartford
STOCKER	S	Sergeant		2 Company Glamorgan RGA (TF) Southern Outfall and Plumstead Common
STOKES	J W G	2nd Lieutenant		5 Company Cornwall RGA (TF) Erith and Dartford
STOOL	S	Gunner		5 Company Cornwall RGA (TF) Erith and Dartford
SULLIVAN		Gunner		3 Company Essex and Suffolk RGA (TF) Purfleet

SYKES	H	Gunner		Not known
TARR	H	Gunner		2 Company Glamorgan RGA (TF) Southern Outfall and Plumstead Common
TAYLOR	Frank Charles	Gunner		Not known
TAYLOR		Sapper		6 Company London Electrical Engineers RE (TF) (Searchlights) North Woolwich
THOMAS	H	Gunner		2 Company Glamorgan RGA (TF) Southern Outfall and Plumstead Common
THOMAS		Gunner		5 Company Cornwall RGA (TF) Erith and Dartford
THOMPSON	J H	Gunner		2 Company Glamorgan RGA (TF) Southern Outfall and Plumstead Common

TREGEARS		Bombardier		5 Company Cornwall RGA (TF) Erith and Dartford
TROAK	E	Gunner		2 Company Glamorgan RGA (TF) Southern Outfall and Plumstead Common
TUBBS	Walter Dean	Gunner		3 Company Essex and Suffolk RGA (TF) Purfleet
TUCKER	T	Gunner		2 Company Glamorgan RGA (TF) Southern Outfall and Plumstead Common
TUCKER	W	Gunner		2 Company Glamorgan RGA (TF) Southern Outfall and Plumstead Common
TURNER		Gunner		Regulars and "K" Army RA Abbey Wood (Lessness Abbey)

VIGAR	P	Gunner		2 Company Glamorgan RGA (TF) Southern Outfall and Plumstead Common
VIGGERS	A	Bombardier		2 Company Glamorgan RGA (TF) Southern Outfall and Plumstead Common
WALKER	J	Lieutenant		2 Company Glamorgan RGA (TF) Southern Outfall and Plumstead Common
WARD	W	Bombardier		2 Company Glamorgan RGA (TF) Southern Outfall and Plumstead Common
WARREN		Gunner		3 Company Essex and Suffolk RGA (TF) Purfleet
WHITE	H	Gunner		2 Company Glamorgan RGA (TF) Southern Outfall and Plumstead

				Common
WILLIAMS	T	Gunner		Cornwall RGA
WILLIAMS	W	Sapper		Tyne Electrical Engineers RA (TF) (Searchlights) Darenth
WILLIAMSON	W	Gunner		2 Company Glamorgan RGA (TF) Southern Outfall and Plumstead Common
WILLIAMSON	W	Sapper		Tyne Electrical Engineers RA (TF) (Searchlights) Darenth
WILSON	R	Lieutenant		Kent RGA (TF) Royal Arsenal Defences
WOOLCOCK	W	Gunner		5 Company Cornwall RGA (TF) Erith and Dartford
WYATT	C	Bombardier		2 Company Glamorgan RGA (TF) Southern Outfall and Plumstead

				Common
YOUNG	J	Gunner		Not known

www.ingramcontent.com/pod-product-compliance
Ingram Content Group UK Ltd.
Pitfield, Milton Keynes, MK11 3LW, UK
UKHW061953290726
14090UKWH00021B/1209

9 780957 604223